YOU'RE —— CLOSER THAN YOU THINK WHETHER YOU REALIZE IT OR NOT ——

JOHNNIE JOHNSON

For permission requests, contact the publisher at:

World Class Coaches®
2300 W. Sahara Ave. #800
Las Vegas, NV 89102
800-314-7713
Fax 702-920-7655

www.movingfamiliesinitiative.com
www.worldclasscoaches.com

Printed in the United States of America

Print ISBN: 978-1-54394-057-2
eBook ISBN: 978-1-54394-058-9

US $19.95

CONTENTS

SECTION 6 — WORKING FROM INSIDE OUT

SECTION 7 — SLOW DOWN LONG ENOUGH SO YOU CAN MOVE FASTER

ACKNOWLEDGMENTS

I give thanks to the good Lord for His grace and for blessing the Johnson household, Johnnie and Julie, with three wonderful children in Kirk Anthony, Collin Wayne, and Camille Marie. We are truly blessed as a family!

I give thanks to my wonderful departed mother, Jessie Mae Johnson, who taught me that life is about successfully navigating and managing transition and change with a focus on your goals, despite certain adverse circumstances.

Furthermore, she taught me that life is about the power of believing—the simple faith that if you want to accomplish something, you must start with a crystal-clear vision, have a purposeful mission driving your goals, put forth your maximum effort, and not be afraid of failure.

I give thanks to the World Class Coaches® team of professionals and to the company's affinity and alliance relationships. We're grateful for the opportunity to assist so many different people around the world through various phases of transition and change in their lives.

I give thanks to my high school algebra teacher, Mrs. Mayer, and my college mentor, Dr. John Butler, as well as to all my other teachers and college professors for helping me grow personally, socially, and in the classroom.

I give thanks to all my former football coaches, specifically Ben Bloomer, Darrel Royal, Fred Akers, Ray Malavasi, John

Robinson, and Chuck Knox — for helping me grow personally on and off the field. I give thanks to my former mentor and life coach, the late Lou Tice, for teaching me that my playing field in life is the world.

INTRODUCTION

Many people have goals in life, whether they realize it or not. And, most people are closer than they think to achieving their goals.

For some people, their goals may be in writing, which is crystal clear to them, and they may have a written plan to assist in achieving them. For others, their goals may not be clear to them at all, and they may be operating without a plan.

Whether we have clearly defined goals or not, one thing is certain for almost everyone. Life is a continual process of transition and change. When the time arises we naturally move to the next phase of our lives, whether we're ready for it or not.

Another thing that is certain for all of us is that when we set out to accomplish our goals in life, we are assured of running into obstacles or barriers that may possibly hinder our ability to achieve them. These potential roadblocks may come in the form of circumstances, some of which may be out of our control. They may also come in the form of things that are not going as planned in our lives or negative comments we hear from others that are not aligned with our goals.

Goal attainment is a process driven by a higher purpose. As we pursue our purpose in life, we achieve our goals, one step at a time. Often, this requires us to have a purpose-driven platform and the focus and direction that will enable us to take the first step, then the next step, one at time, and will put us in the best position to achieve our goals despite the circumstances. This may be a challenge for some of us because of our general situation.

There are many factors that drive these natural changes in our lives or the lives of our loved ones. *You're Closer Than You Think Whether You Realize It or Not* is about successfully navigating and managing these natural phases of transition and change in our lives, one step at a time. With each step, we move closer to achieving our overall goals in life.

The purpose of this book is to assist you and your entire family to create a purpose-driven platform to help you to tap into your natural competitive spirit in order to overcome obstacles or barriers standing in the way of your achieving your goals in life. Specifically, I'm referring to the challenges that can get in your way when you're going through natural periods of transition and change in your life.

If you're a parent, a specific focus is placed on your children. That focus extends to your children's grandparents, their aunts and uncles, and their cousins as they journey through the natural phases of transition and change in their lives as well.

Another one of the aims of the book is to encourage and inspire you to remain focused on your goals, and remain confident in your ability to achieve them, one step at a time, despite certain circumstances, setbacks, doubts, or fears you may encounter in life.

Bottom line, you're closer than you think to achieving your goals in life whether you realize it or not. Now it's time for you to take the next step, and then the next step, until you achieve them.

DEDICATION

A number of circumstances driving the changes in the lives of parents, especially those with young children, may cause them to move or relocate their family. They're in search of a higher purpose or seeking to meet the needs of their family with the move.

This book is dedicated to the parents and the approximately 10 million children, ages 19 and younger, who move or relocate annually throughout the United States according to the U.S. Census.

World Class Coaches® serves as the facilitator of the Moving Families Initiative (MFI). Our aim with the Initiative is to assist parents who are moving or relocating by making the move less stressful for their entire family. A specific focus is placed on assisting their children, ages 19 and younger, in dealing with the physical and emotional challenges of changing neighborhoods, schools, and friends, whether they're moving across town or across the country.

We're committed to serving, protecting, and meeting the needs of the parents' entire family during periods of transition and change throughout their lifetime.

Our commitment to serving the parents' entire families, with a specific focus on their children, extends to the kid's grandparents, their aunts and uncles, and their cousins, as they too, go through periods of transition and change in their lives.

Our overall aim of the MFI is to provide families access to the following when they move or relocate:

- High quality education
- Children's extracurricular activities
- Affordable housing
- Economic opportunities.

You will hear more about all four overall aims later on. For now, be aware that children's participation in extracurricular activities provides them with a platform on which to build character and enhance life skills and values that they may find difficult to learn elsewhere. Their participation can also assist them in developing new friendships on a safe platform when they move to a new neighborhood or school.

These core tenets are contributing factors to why we encourage kids to be involved with an extracurricular activity of their choice.

One of our aims with the MFI is for all eligible children, ages 19 and younger, to be involved with an extracurricular activity of their choice when they move or relocate to a new school or neighborhood. We're not concerned about which activity it is as long as they're involved in one of their choosing.

To assist in the attainment of this goal, a portion of the proceeds from the sale of this book will go to the Moving Families Initiative Extracurricular Activities Scholarship Plan. The plan provides scholarships to cover children ages 19 and younger participation fees for involvement in an extracurricular activity of their choice when they move or relocate to a new neighborhood or school. Young children of parents moving or relocating at all social and economic income levels are eligible for the scholarships to help welcome kids to their new home, school, or community.

1

SECTION

START WHERE YOU ARE

I was raised by a single parent, the late Jessie Mae, in a poor family of 11 kids in La Grange, Texas. My mom instilled strong values, character, and life skills in her children as we grew up. She was the single greatest influence in my life. She continues to inspire the mission, purpose, and vision in my life today.

Outside of my mom, the greatest positive influences in my life while growing up as a kid came from teachers, coaches, and school counselors. One of the most significant impacts came from Mrs. Mayer, my algebra teacher at La Grange High School.

Early in my school years, I struggled in math. I did not see myself as being very good in the subject while growing up as a kid, that was until I got into Mrs. Mayer's algebra class. In addition to my mom, I credit her for being one of the most important people instrumental in preparing me to take steps to put myself in a position to achieve my goals in life.

The ironic thing was that prior to my taking her class, word around our school was that "You better hope you don't get Mrs. Mayer because she was such a hard teacher." Well, that was my hope – not to get her; however, God had another plan for me. I got Mrs. Mayer for algebra.

The two facts that I did not see myself as being good in math and that I was assigned to Mrs. Mayer's class just about caused me to think that I might never make it through school. That was until she saw me walking down the hallway before classes began on the first day of school and informed me she would like to speak to me about her class in her classroom.

As I nervously entered her classroom, she looked at me and said, "Johnnie, I understand you're a really good football player," to which I barely responded. She went on to say, "I want you to know that I expect you to give me the same level of commitment and effort in my class that you give your coaches on the football field."

I not only gave great effort on the football field, I was firmly committed to playing the game. It's where I felt most comfortable. Prior to taking her class, I had set a goal for the future to play in the National Football League. To accomplish that goal, I would need to first qualify to play college football, so that also became one of my goals.

Mrs. Mayer was a demanding teacher. She gave homework every day, and on some days, every student in the class had to answer one of the questions on the homework from the prior night out loud to the rest of the class. If one of my classmates failed to give the correct answer, I became one of two students who were called upon to give the correct answer to the class.

Despite my belief that I was not good in math when I began the course and under Mrs. Mayer's guidance as a teacher, I went on to earn an "A" in algebra that year.

Unbeknownst to me at the time, I had taken a step toward achieving one my goals. You see algebra was one of the core subjects I needed to pass to qualify for college admission.

I start with this story as a tribute to Mrs. Mayer and all the teachers, coaches, and school counselors around the world like her.

CHAPTER 1

WHY ARE YOU HERE?

When I was 13 years old growing up as a teenager in La Grange, Texas, I recall a series of conversations I had with my mom about our family situation. I was old enough to be aware of our circumstances.

My parents were separated. They were later divorced. That left my mom to raise 5 of their 11 children alone. My mother dedicated her life to raising her children to the best of her ability with the few resources she had to work with. One resource was government-assistance programs. I grew up on the welfare system.

Needless to say, this was a difficult time for me and all my siblings. Kids really need someone they can count on in life, and for me that person was my mother. She was always there for us kids with love and patience. Despite our circumstances, we knew we could always count on her love and leadership.

Each family member had specific chores to do, and mom made it very clear that the rest of the family was relying on each of us to fulfill our family responsibilities. Although we all had specific chores, one thing was very evident to me: my mother led by example. She was the first one up in the morning every day, and the last one to bed every night. She worked constantly in between to provide for and support the family.

Seeing how hard my mom worked inspired me to take a summer job as a farmhand. I felt the need to provide more financial assistance and to boost her efforts. On pay day, I would take the money I earned and give it to her to help provide for the family.

These were stressful times for the whole family. I could feel the pressures squarely on my shoulders. So much so that it got to the point where I felt like I could not take it anymore. These burdens led to a series of valued conversations with my mom, and one of those revolved around the importance of having a mission and vision in life despite your circumstances.

I vividly recall her saying, "Son, God has a plan for you. He placed you here for a reason. It's important for you to find out why He placed you here. And what your purpose is in life.

"When you look around and see what's going on in your life today, you can easily become discouraged. It's easy to get all wrapped up in the chaos going on in your life.

"However, those things should not drive you. Figure out your mission and vision in life and be strong and of good courage in pursuing them despite your circumstances or negative comments you hear from other people." She was summarizing several Scriptures she had read from the Bible.

Initially, all the mission and vision talk went right over my head. However, one thing I learned from my mom was that God does not place limitations on any of us; we either place them on ourselves or we allow others to place them on us.

When I look back, Mom planted a seed, which led me to begin thinking about why I was here on earth. And despite our circumstances, it was up to me to figure out my purpose in life.

CHAPTER 2

WHAT IS YOUR MISSION, VISION, AND PURPOSE?

Mom's words of encouragement sounded good. However, although I knew it was up to me to figure out why God placed me here, I was having a hard time seeing through our circumstances. This led me to ask my mom about her mission and vision in life.

When I did, she replied in a calm and confident manner, "God put me here for you kids," she said. "I envision raising my kids to be the best that they can be and someday living in a brick home with a clothes line hanging between two large oak trees in the back yard. And on the clothes line, I envision clothes blowing and drying in the wind during all seasons of the year."

When I heard her comments, I recall thinking to myself, "When was the last time the United States government purchased one person a brick home?" Based on our situation, I felt that would be the only way we would ever have such a home.

Although those were my thoughts about her owning a brick home, I was fascinated by the fact that she could envision such a bright future with such clarity, since she was just recently divorced and receiving government assistance to help feed her kids.

However, I took her advice and tried to remain strong because that is what I needed just to get by on a daily basis.

As I continued to take my mom's advice, I noticed that my attitude started to change. I began to have a more positive outlook on life, even though I was not certain what was really driving the change.

As my attitude continued to change for the better, I started to develop a genuine interest in sports. That led me to deciding to take part in sports when I transitioned to Junior High School. I played football, basketball, and I participated in track and field.

Something else occurred during this process. I discovered I had been blessed with exceptional athletic skills. I realized I was a good athlete.

With my mom's words of encouragement ringing in my mind and my sincere interest in sports, I made two of the best decisions of my life. They were when I set a goal as a teenager to play pro football and when I chose sports over drugs, alcohol, and gangs. Although no one from La Grange had played in the National Football League before, that was my first vision.

My vision caused me to replay some of the conversations I had with my mom over and over again in my head. One thing I recall was that my vision was just as clear to me as my Mom's mission of raising her kids to be the best they could be and her vision of someday living in a brick home was to her.

I could clearly see myself playing in the National Football League. I could see myself as a professional football player with such clarity that at times I felt I was actually taking part in an NFL game. In fact, I often visualized myself participating in the games.

Although I could not see the "why" for my purpose in life at that moment, I decided to put my vision and goals in writing and review them daily. This step brought more clarity and focus to those targets in my life.

Something else was starting to emerge, which I was not aware of at the time. When I put my vision and goals in writing and took time to review them daily and used the techniques of imagery and visualization, I began the process of developing and practicing some of the success habit patterns of highly effective people.

Although I was not aware of my true purpose in life at the time, I began the process of creating the success platform used by many highly effective and successful people in all facets of life.

One of the most significant things that occurred during that time period that coincided with the beginning of the creation of a purpose-driven success platform in my life was that I signed up to play football in junior high school.

When I did, although it seemed like I was a million miles away from my vision, I took a step toward achieving my goal of playing pro football. Ironically, I was closer than I thought to attainting my goal than I realized at the time. Today, I understand why; that's because many of us are closer than we think to achieving our goals in life whether we realize it or not. All we need to do is take the next appropriate step in our lives. And then the next one.

CHAPTER 3

BE THE BEST YOU CAN BE

When I look back on my life today, I now realize just how fortu-nate I was growing up as a kid. I was blessed because of my mom and people like Mrs. Mayer, my algebra teacher at La Grange High School. They were two people who appeared to be different in many ways, yet both had one thing in common: their expectations of the children in their lives.

In my Mom's case, it was her kids she was raising at home. In Mrs. Mayer's case, it was the kids she was teaching at school. The expectations both had of us was that we were going to be the best we could be.

In talking to my mom, I recall a conversation in which she said, "We're all blessed in different ways. Son, you've started to recognize some of your gifts." She was referring to my interest in sports and my discovery that I had been blessed with exceptional athletic gifts.

I also recall her saying to me, "Regardless of your situation, all I ask of you is to just be yourself, but be the best you can be, despite your circumstances." It was part of my mom's mission to raise her kids to be the best that they could be in their lives.

When I look back today, this is precisely what Mrs. Mayer was communicating to me when she said: "Johnnie, I understand you're a really good football player. I expect you to give me the same level of commitment and effort in my class, that you give your coaches on the football field." She was communicating her expectations of me to simply be the best I could be, despite my circumstances.

Although I viewed my mom and Mrs. Mayer as not knowing much about sports, their comments were consistent with what I was also starting to hear from my coaches.

When Ben Bloomer, my high school head football coach, first informed me that he had decided that I had the ability to play on the varsity team as a freshman, he asked if this was something I would like to pursue. When I replied yes, he then said, "All I want from you is to be your best self." He was saying to be the best you can be despite being a freshman playing on the varsity team.

When we look back in life, there are a lot of things that come and go, and then there are others that are life-changing.

In my case, there were three people, my mom, Mrs. Mayer, and Coach Bloomer, all of whom appeared to be so different but who were communicating one common message to me at a time when I needed it the most. To me, that was truly life-changing and meant you should be the best you can be whether at home, in the classroom, or on the football field. It really hit home with me.

Although I felt inspired by the common message of encouragement, I still felt an almost unbearable amount of pressure in my life. That's because one thing for certain had not changed in my life, and that was my circumstances at home. Add in my having to compete as a freshman on the varsity in football, and it all appeared to be more than I could handle with this new challenge.

This led to another series of conversations with my mom, during one of which she shared the following scripture with me:

Matthew 5: 14-16: "You are the light of the world. A city that is set on a hill cannot be hidden. Nor do they light a lamp and put it under a basket, but on a lamp stand, and it gives light to all who are in the house. Let your light so shine before men, that they may see your good works and glorify your Father in heaven."

She then said, "I ask that you do only one thing: Do everything within your power to please God by letting your light shine."

Her words really hit home with me. Based on my belief in the God-given talents I was discovering I had, with my mom's encouragement, Mrs. Mayer's belief in me, and the confidence Coach Bloomer showed in me, I decided that there was a way I could honor God.

I said to myself, "In football, I can best glorify Him for granting me these gifts and talents by approaching each and every play in sports, whether it be practice or a game, with every ounce of energy and drive I have in my body — and let Him take care of the rest."

Whatever happened would be up to Him, but I was going to do my part by playing the game at the highest level possible at all times, regardless of the circumstances. I decided that even though I might not be able to control the circumstances, I could control my approach to them. I was not going to allow circumstances or the comments I heard from others knock me off my goal.

I decided I was also going to take the same approach in the classroom at school and at home. I knew it would not be easy, but I decided that the best way to glorify God was to take this approach in all areas of my life.

Although I was unable to see it at the time, that was the encouragement I was receiving from my mom, Mrs. Mayer, and Coach Bloomer. It was then up to me to stay committed to being "the best I can be" despite my circumstances. I accepted that commitment.

Equipped with this new positive attitude in life, opportunities and possibilities started to emerge as I began to transition through high school. Attending college started to become more of a possibility. This became evident when as a sophomore, I received my first piece of recruiting literature—a questionnaire from the University of Notre Dame!

This was the first of many such recruiting inquiries I would receive in four different sports during my high school career.

As I continued to take steps to transition through high school from my freshman year, to my sophomore, then junior, and ultimately my senior year, it became very clear to me that I was going through a natural period of development and change in my life. I was going through it whether I was ready for it or not.

Something else occurred during this time: it became clear that I would have an opportunity to qualify for college on an athletic scholarship. However, to be awarded one, I would need to qualify academically as well. This is where I thank Mrs. Mayer once again.

Math is a core subject in high school. Most colleges require you to have taken and passed a required number of core subjects in high school to qualify for both admission into college and an athletic scholarship award. Math is one of those core subjects.

In my case, I consider myself to be very fortunate that Mrs. Mayer taught me algebra when she did. She not only helped me overcome my beliefs about not being good in math, but she also aided me in gaining the required core credits I needed to achieve one of my goals — to go to college on an athletic scholarship.

All of these great opportunities that were emerging were also bringing on another major challenge for me. With all the college choices to select from, I was going to be faced with a couple of major decisions. One would be which college would I attend, and the other would be which sport would I play in college — football, basketball, baseball, or participate in track and field?

By my senior year I had received communication and scholarship offers from over 100 different colleges and universities from around the country.

This is when I made one of the best decisions I've made in my life. That's when I chose to attend the University of Texas at Austin to play football as a student-athlete on a full athletic scholarship.

I had achieved my goal of going to college to play football. Off to Austin!

Initially, my transition from La Grange to Austin and from high school to college turned out to be a difficult one. This was the first time I had to move or relocate to a new city, school, or community.

Many of the challenges I faced revolved around my adapting to a new city and the college life. It was the first time I was away from home, and I really missed my family and friends.

Although I was homesick, there was one place where I felt right at home in college. That was when I was around my new teammates on the Texas Longhorn football team.

I'm a big believer in children's participating in an activity of their choice when they move or relocate. It provides them with a platform on which to build character and enhance life skills and values. It can also assist them in developing new friendships in a safe environment. The fact that I was a member of the Longhorn football team played a role in my making a successful transition to Austin and the University of Texas.

One of the most difficult challenges I faced in adjusting to college was missing my mom. I was constantly worried about her and my remaining three brothers and sisters who were still at home with her. Although I was off at college, I knew the circumstances back at home had not changed.

There was one thing that had changed for me. I could now add my college football coaches, Darrel Royal and Fred Akers, and Professor Dr. John Butler and others to the list of people encouraging me to be the best I can be, despite the circumstances.

Coach Royal and Coach Akers were instrumental in my development on and off the field as a person and an athlete. Dr. Butler was instrumental in my settling into campus life as a student and in settling into the community. I was very fortunate to have the three of them play the role they played in my life during my college career.

At the University of Texas, I was twice selected as an All-American defensive back, and I was projected to be a #1 draft pick in the annual National Football League player draft. My vision of playing in the NFL was about to be realized.

That projection became a reality when I became a #1 draft pick of the Los Angeles Rams. Although I had looked forward to that moment since I was a teenager growing up in La Grange, when it finally occurred, I was stunned. I was speechless, although I had just achieved my childhood goal of having the opportunity to play in the National Football League.

CHAPTER 4

VISION BECOMES REALITY

Life is a continual process of transition and change. When the time arises, we naturally move to the next phase of our lives, whether we're ready for it or not. That's the case when I look back on my life.

It seems like I went from elementary, to junior high, to high school and then to college in a flash. And it seemed like I no longer arrived on the University of Texas campus as a freshman when I realized I was then a senior. It seemed like the moment I arrived on campus my college career was over, and it was time for me to transition on to the next phase of my life. That was on to the NFL.

The time arose when I received a phone call from the Los Angeles Rams informing me they had just drafted me in the first round of the National Football League draft.

At that very moment, I thought about all the conversations I had with my Mom growing up as a young teenager. I just could not thank her enough for providing me with the guidance, inspiration, and the encouragement to stay focused on my goals when so many things existed that could have easily gotten in the way.

When I arrived in Los Angeles and signed my rookie contract with the Rams, opportunities continued to flow my way. As the team's first million-dollar player, I was overwhelmed with the thought and joy of finally being able to achieve another of the goals I set as a 13 year old — that goal was to purchase my mom a home. I had made a decision that the first money I earned from playing pro football was going to go toward purchasing her that brick home she envisioned.

That day soon arrived. When I returned to La Grange shortly after signing my NFL contract, I was able to purchase my mom the brick home she dreamed about.

Words cannot really express the joy and peace I experienced when I presented her with the keys to her new home and thanked her for dedicating her life's purpose to raising her kids to be the best they could be, despite overwhelming odds.

I looked her right in the eyes and told her, "Mom, you have done enough in your life. Now it is our turn as your children to take care of you. I don't want you to have to worry about anything the rest of your life." With many of her words ringing in my ears, I left for Los Angeles to begin the next phase of my life: my rookie year in the National Football League.

One of the most difficult challenges I faced after being drafted by the Rams took place when I moved from Austin to Los Angeles. It was difficult enough leaving a university, a city, and my teammates and friends behind and moving to a place where I didn't really know anyone. To compound matters, I needed to adjust to the size of the city of Los Angeles. It was a cultural shock to me in all aspects of life.

Just as I had experienced in my move from La Grange to Austin, there was one place where I immediately felt right at home in Los Angeles: that was when I was around my new teammates on the Los Angeles football team.

As previously mentioned, I'm a believer in children's participating in an activity of their choice when they move or relocate. It provides them with a platform on which to build character and enhance life skills and values and also assists them in developing new friendships in a safe environment.

That was definitely the case in my moving from La Grange to Austin, Texas. And that was most certainly the case in my moving from Austin, Texas, to Los Angeles, California. My being a member of the Los Angeles Rams football team played a major role in my adjusting to the Los Angeles area successfully for the beginning of my National Football League career.

I began my NFL career by setting a goal to play for 10 years in the league. At the time, the average player's career lasted only 3 1/2 years. To assist me in achieving that goal, I decided to identify those precious few players who had done what I was seeking to accomplish and to find out as much about them as I possibly could. I looked to seasoned veterans who had been around for 8, 10, or 12 years, seeking to learn everything I could find out about them.

I wanted to know about their lifestyle, practice habits, work ethic, their approach to the game, and their thought patterns. Most of all I wanted to know how they dealt with difficult circumstances in their lives, which could get in the way of the achievement of their goals. I also wanted to know how they dealt with situations in which things did not go as they planned and how they dealt with negative comments from critics. But most of all, I wanted to know what really made them tick — what was really driving them.

I was not only interested in studying long-term NFL players who had been playing in the league for a decade or more, I was also interested in studying the lifestyles and thought patterns of the billionaire owners. I also wanted to study the companies that were willing to spend millions of dollars advertising their products, services, and brands with NFL teams.

When I look back, I cannot necessarily tell you what prompted me to take these steps when I arrived in the NFL. However, I'm certain it revolved around some of the conversations I had with my mom, specifically, those in which she encouraged me to be the best I can be in whatever it is I'm pursuing in life and to figure out why God put me there – my purpose in life.

Even though I had achieved one of my goals of having an opportunity to play in the NFL, I had not figured out my purpose in life yet. As I look back, what's interesting is although I had not determined my life's purpose at that time, I was crystal clear about one thing; I knew God did not put me here just to be a football player. I was convinced God had a higher purpose for me, and it was up to me to find out what it was.

While studying the billionaire owners and world-class athletes, I discovered that many of them approached life and the game of football in the same or similar manner in which I was conditioned to think by my mom and the other mentors in my life. I noticed that we shared similar thought patterns. Most of all, I noticed that many of them had had to overcome difficult backgrounds or cir-cumstances and deal with doubts expressed by others that could have knocked them off their goals.

I often wondered, "What drives these people?" I decided I was going to be on a constant search to find the answers. I felt that approach would better enable me to not only realize my goal of playing 10 years in the NFL but also assist me in figuring out my purpose in life.

After my first year in the National Football League, a defin-ing moment occurred in my life. I went back to Texas to visit my mom at her new home. As I was walking through the house, giv-ing thanks for the small things that I always desired for her such as central heating and air conditioning, I walked into the dining room and paused for a moment. When I looked through the din-ing room window into the backyard, I noticed two large oak trees. Hanging between them was a clothes line, and on it were clothes that looked just like they did back in the old days. Clothes on a clothes line were normal back in my mom's days when I was grow-ing up as child. For me to see it at that moment, all I could do was just stand there and stare at what was before my eyes. As I stared at the clothes, I reflected back on the obstacles and barriers that stood between my mom's circumstances and her vision. I was curious to know how she remained focused on her vision when it appeared the world was crashing in on her.

This prompted many different emotions and thoughts and even more questions: How did she do it without being knocked off her goal? Why is it that more people do not approach their lives in a similar manner? And how could I help others to realize the inner peace, self-satisfaction, and self-fulfillment I was experiencing at that moment?

Of all the things that have transpired in my life, the conversation I had with my mom at age 13 — when she confidently described her vision and mission to me in the midst of what I personally saw as a world of chaos, helped me develop my belief system. Witnessing the clothes hanging on the clothes line between the oak trees in my mom's backyard approximately 10 years later inspired my life's mission.

Although part of her vision was realized through me, her son, I still wondered how she was able to stay true to her mission and vision in life, despite the many overwhelming circumstances, obstacles, and barriers standing between her and her vision. When I inquired she simply replied, "I was placed here for you kids, to be the best mother I could be. My mission in life was to raise my kids to be the best that they can be."

Her comments echoed what she had said 10 years earlier when I was just a teenager. But then she added: "When I look back on my life, I feel a lot of joy for the special blessings that have come to me for being true to my purpose in life."

She continued, "When you look around and see what's going on in your life today, the only things that have changed — other than the fact that you're older and wiser — are your circumstances. And just as it was easy to get all wrapped up in the adverse circumstances surrounding the way you grew up, it is just as easy to allow the success you are experiencing today to go to your head so that you lose sight of how you got there."

Mothers keep you grounded. She then predicted, "Just as you faced difficult situations, chaos, and choices early in your life, you will face others as you get older. The key will be how you handle them."

Her comments caused me to have a greater desire to keep focused on my vision and mission in life and to be on a constant search for the most effective ways to realize them. It is a part of my mission in life to share this goal with as many people as I can reach and touch with this life-changing education.

Mother, I thank you, and hope to honor your blessed memory and to serve God by letting my light shine bright. Of all my life coaches, you were the first and the best.

Start Where You Are	Success Habit Patterns					

SUCCESS HABIT PATTERNS

I found studying world-class athletes and other highly effective people fascinating. I found studying billionaire team owners and the companies that advertise with their teams equally fascinating. One of the first things you notice about both groups is that they share similar success habit patterns and principles of thought and behavior. And they're driven by a strong natural and healthy competitive spirit.

As I came in contact with more highly effective people, I observed that they were often driven by a strong mission and purpose in life. They had a clear vision of what they were pursuing, and they were consistent in their ability to remain focused on their goals despite running into twists, turns, and roadblocks along the way.

Over the years, I have learned more about how they were able to achieve this remarkable feat despite encountering circumstances that could potentially cause them to give up on their goals.

In this section, I will review what I have learned about success habit patterns and principles. This is of great value because many of us are susceptible to being knocked off our goals when we go through various phases of transition and change in our lives or when we encounter life's challenges.

CHAPTER 5

SUCCESS PATTERNS

I consider myself to be very fortunate. I feel blessed because over the course of my life I've had a chance to team with, compete against, be around, and study many highly effective people across all sectors of society. To assist us in better understanding them, I would like to share some of what I've learned from studying the success patterns of highly effective people.

Over the years, I've met many different people from all sectors of society who have overcome many obstacles or barriers in life and achieved an incredible amount of success. For some, the success came quickly and at an early age. For others, it came later in life.

Whether success came early or late, one of the success patterns highly effective people possess is their resolve and unique ability to tap into their healthy competitive spirit when needed. We will talk more about our competitive spirit later, but for now just know that male or female, old or young, or regardless of where we fall on the socio-economic scale, we all are competitive by nature.

Highly effective people often tap into their competitive spirit to assist them in remaining focused on their goals when they encounter obstacles or barriers that could potentially affect their ability to achieve them. Their ability to stay focused on their goals despite dealing with challenges better enables them to consistently put themselves in a position for success in realizing more of their goals.

For some, their resolve and ability to persist and attain their goals seems to provide them with a certain level of inner peace, self-satisfaction, and self-fulfillment that many of us desire in life, especially when we know we have given it our all. Whether we succeeded at the time or not was not nearly as important as knowing we could lay our head down on our pillows each night knowing we gave it our best shot.

As I came to know more highly effective people, I observed that they, too, had a unique ability to remain focused on their goals despite encountering things that could potentially hinder their ability to do so. The more I observed, the more I wanted to know about how they could be so focused in spite of encountering obstacles or barriers in their lives.

In search of finding out more, I specifically focused on the successful habit patterns of world-class athletes. When I arrived in the NFL, I set a goal to play for 10 years. I set that goal although players' careers lasted only 3.5 years in the League on average.

To assist me in achieving my goal, I wanted to learn more about the success patterns of players who had played in the league for 8,10, or 12 years or more. The better I understood and practiced and imitated the success strategies utilized by many of these greats of the game, the better I could position myself to achieve more of my goals in sports and in life.

One of the first success patterns I observed from these highly effective, long-term veterans of the NFL revolved around the definition of proper versus improper goal setting.

The men I was studying all had had long pro football careers and had played for 8 to 12 years or more in the NFL. Because of the longevity of their careers, I was curious to know more about the contributing factors to why most NFL players' careers lasted on average only 3.5 years.

Since the careers of the men I was studying spanned an 8- to 12-year period, that meant that a lot of other players' careers were lasting only one or two years in order to keep the average NFL player's career at 3.5 years.

Although there are numerous other contributing factors involved, such as high-level competition and career-ending injuries, there's a real interesting one that contributes to players' careers lasting only an average of 3.5 years: that factor is improper goal setting.

Many players set a goal to merely get to the NFL and do not commit to play a certain number of years once they get there. As a result, once they get there they lose their focus. They do not approach playing the sport with the same level of commitment and resolve that played a major role in their approach to achieving their goal of getting there.

This form of improper or careless goal setting will cause them to lose their passion, drive, and motivation for playing the game at the professional level. As a result, they become more susceptible to obstacles or barriers that can potentially knock them off their goal, including being beaten out by other players who are competing for their jobs.

That was definitely not the case with the group I was studying. Many of them shared similar success patterns. That's not unusual, since many highly effective people do. However, there was something unique about this group. You could see, feel, and hear the passion revolving around their setting their goals properly and their commitment to them.

Proper goal setting is when you not only set a goal for yourself, let's say to get to the NFL, but it's also when you set a goal to get there and play for 5 years or any other number. When setting the goal properly, the total number of years is not nearly as important as setting a firm goal to play a specific number of years with a sincere commitment.

In other words, proper goal setting is an ongoing process. It's about setting goals beyond the initial target you've established and achieved for yourself. It's about sincerely committing to your aims beyond the goals you've already accomplished with all the drive, motivation, and passion you have in your body. It's a success pattern practiced by many highly effective people across all sectors of society.

A better understanding of the success patterns of this group led me to take another step. I began studying the success patterns of world-class athletes as compared with other highly effective people across all sectors of society. What I discovered is that highly effective people across all spectrums and professions share similar success patterns or characteristics.

One of my objectives in life was to be on a constant search to better understand these success patterns and see how they apply to me and to you. The better I understand and can practice these patterns personally, the better I can position myself to achieve more of my goals in life; again, this is despite encountering the natural twists, turns, and roadblocks I run into that could potentially hinder my ability to achieve my goals in life. The same applies to you.

Over the years I've discovered that highly effective people share five success patterns or characteristics:

1. **They share similar thought patterns**. They have a unique way of thinking. Many of them use positive thought patterns and critical thinking skills to assist them in remaining focused on their goals when they encounter obstacles or barriers in their life.

2. **They believe in a higher power**. They're driven by a higher purpose. And they remain faithful to their beliefs in tough times.

3. **They are end-results oriented.** They're goal-oriented. They faithfully begin the process of

accomplishing their intentions to succeed by keeping the end in mind. They begin with a clearly defined mission and vision. Their goals are purpose-driven. They desire to improve their skill-set daily with a strong commitment to be the best they can be.

4. **They take daily, incremental action steps.** They develop a specific action plan. They engage in disciplined thoughts and take disciplined, incremental action steps to arrive at their goals, one step at a time.

5. **When a problem arises, they first look to refocus on the desired target**. When problems arise, they look for solutions. They "lock on" to the desired outcome and "lock out" the chaos that may be contributing to the challenges they're facing.

Often when I share my findings regarding world-class athletes and highly effective people, some folks have difficulty relating to them. They have a tendency to think that members from these groups possess special gifts, talents, or character traits that somehow they do not have. Their perception is that these highly effective people have been blessed with special gifts and talents in a way that excludes them.

During the latter part of my professional football career, I studied the psychological characteristics of some of the world's greatest performing athletes as compared to peak performers in other professions. Part of my study was focused on highly effective real estate sales people. My focus was to discover the basic differences in the thought processes between the two groups, but what I discovered was that both groups shared similar thought patterns related to success.

Once again, when I shared my findings regarding the similarities between these groups some people did not see the relevance to them because, again, they believed that members of both groups had been blessed in a way that excluded them. In other words, they had some reason to justify why the athlete or elite sales professional was performing at a level that was not available to them. They felt limited based on what they perceived to be things beyond their abilities.

As I reflected on this, it reminded me of how we sometimes limit ourselves by the way we see, think, feel, or act. Our perception is determined by the lens through which we see the world. And how we see things plays a vital role in how we think, feel, and act and what we expect in life.

Many of us may find ourselves in a similar situation and later wonder, "What happened? Where did we go wrong?" Well, we can start with the lens through which we see the world, and how we see things based on the way we've been conditioned to think.

No matter how great our desire to achieve our goals in life, if we're looking through the wrong set of lenses, we may unintentionally knock ourselves off our goal. No matter how hard we try or how much we believe in the resources, our ability to be effective in achieving our goals is greatly affected by the lens with which we view the world. You may ask, "Why is that?"

We have a natural filtering system that enables us to filter things through our senses of touch, smell, taste, hearing, and sight. This process is affected by our past experiences and by the authority figures in our lives. We forever perceive the world around us based on how we have been conditioned to think.

Our filtering system may be impacted or affected by our environment, especially when we go through periods of transition and change in our lives. It may also be affected when we move or relocate to a new city, community, state, or country.

As we seek to know what feasible steps we may take to develop the success patterns of highly effective people, it is crucial for us to become more aware of how our perceptions are formed, how they affect the way we see the world, and the role they play in the way we think and act.

To remain focused on our goals, we will want to become more aware of the role conditioning plays in the formation of our perceptions. The beliefs, habits, attitudes, and expectations we hold today are based on the way we have been conditioned to think.

If we are to remain focused on our goals in the middle of the challenges we face, we must continually assess why we see things, believe things, and do things the way we do. We must be aware that "how we see the world" affects how we interpret the world.

Highly effective people have a way of seeing the world in a manner consistent with their ability to achieve their goals despite certain circumstances in their lives. They do so one step at time. With each step taken, they move closer to achieving their overall goals.

CHAPTER 6

THE BENEFITS OF A HEALTHY COMPETITIVE SPIRIT

I feel blessed in my life. Many of the reasons why revolve around my life experiences that have inspired my mission and purpose in life.

Another reason why I feel blessed is because all three of my children from the Johnson household — Kirk, Collin, and Camille — chose to participate in various extracurricular activities while growing up as kids. They continued participating in these important activities throughout their entire high school careers. Each one would go on to follow in my footsteps and attend college at the University of Texas at Austin on athletic scholarships; Kirk and Collin in football, and Camille in track and field.

Like most parents, it's my desire that they have a greater life than I experienced. The thing I am most intrigued about each of them is their desire to create their own paths in life. Although Kirk, Collin and Camille chose to follow in my footsteps and attend the

University of Texas, neither wanted or welcomed the perception that they were receiving any special benefits because of my having been a Hall of Fame football player at the school. It was their desire to earn every stripe on their own. This was a clear sign of their healthy competitive spirit on display.

This approach will continue to serve them well throughout life. That's because they will continue to run into their own twists, turns, and roadblocks along the path to the attainment of the objectives in their lives. And when they do, when applied constructively, their competitive spirit will assist them in dealing positively with many of these obstacles or barriers.

We're accustomed to seeing people display their competitive spirit in the sports world. In fact, that's one of the contributing factors that's enabled male and female athletes at all levels to become the great performers they've become in their respective sports.

However, we're all competitive by nature. One of my greatest personal traits happens to be my competitive spirit. I'm a highly competitive person, although you may not necessarily know it just by being around me. I learned part of my competitive spirit from my mom when I was growing up as a kid and enhanced it mightily by my many years of playing sports, and more specifically during my 10-year NFL football career. I used that competitiveness to aid me in being the best I could be in the sports world. But I also tap into it today to assist me in being the best I can be at what I am doing and to aid me in dealing with the natural twists, turns, and roadblocks I run into in my everyday life.

My wife Julie has a healthy competitive spirit, and, our three children may be the most competitive members of the family, with Camille being the most competitive of the group. There's no doubt that our children inherited part of their healthy competitive spirit from their parents.

I understand that being known to be competitive can have an unpleasant meaning in some sectors of society. In fact, it's not unusual to feel uncomfortable with our competitiveness. This is understandable because competition affects each of us in different ways. Competing in general makes some of us fairly uncomfortable.

However, having a healthy competitive spirit is good for all of us. It's often more about us being the best we can be and providing an edge to assist us in overcoming obstacles or barriers in our lives than winning a race or coming in first in a competition. Our competitive feelings are an indication of our desire to be the best we can be. It's about putting ourselves in the best position to achieve our goals in life in spite of adverse circumstances. One of the logical triggers to the release of this spirit is a twist, turn or roadblock, or an obstacle or barrier that may be standing in our path to the attainment of our goals.

Therefore, having a healthy competitive spirit is about building a purposeful platform, one in which it's important to understand the context we're operating in when we tap into it. When we take this step, we typically tap into a set of emotions that provide us with great drive, motivation, and energy. This in turn leads to shifting our focus to wanting to be the best we can be and accomplishing our goals despite circumstances we may encounter along the way.

Context and healthy competitive spirit are key. That's because we can be best friends with someone but when we tap into our competitive spirit we will compete against them like they are our most potent enemy. I had this experience firsthand and often during my football career. That's when I competed against some of my best friends who played on rival teams. Before the game, we were best friends, and during the game we competed against each other as bitter rivals. After the game we were best friends again.

During the game our focus was on taking steps to put our respective teams in the best position to win the game. This is why understanding context is so important when it comes to our competitive spirit.

When we tap into our competitive spirit, the feelings can be directed at anyone. This means not just our best friend but perhaps toward an attractive coworker or anyone else or situation that triggers those feelings.

What's important is for us to acknowledge that we've tapped into our competitive spirit when it's triggered. When we fail to do so in everyday life, we are more likely to become cynical. This may come in the form of jealousy acted out by putting someone else down or simply wanting what they have if it's something we've been striving for ourselves.

For example, if our boss was to acknowledge a coworker for a job well done, we may think, "Wait, I want that recognition. I work harder than that person." We may turn against our coworker, by saying things like, "He or she doesn't deserve that recognition. They don't work nearly as hard as I do. Or, why am I trying as hard as I do at this company when the boss' favorite person gets all the rewards?" It is in this context that we want to be very careful with our competitiveness. It can trigger an unhealthy competitive spirit in us.

Having said that, any time these thought processes start to emerge, they let us know we're competitive and they let us know that we've tapped into our competitive spirit. It's important to understand the context driving our competitiveness.

Taking this step will enable us to refocus on our overall goals that we're pursuing in life. When we can channel these feelings into being more motivated and inspired to work harder to overcome any obstacles or barriers standing in the way of achieving our overall goals, then we're using our competitive spirit to our benefit.

The key is understanding that goal attainment is a process driven by a higher purpose. As we pursue our purpose in life we achieve our goals one step at a time. Often, it requires us to have a purpose-driven platform and the focus and direction that will enable us to take the first step, then the next step, one at time, in order to put ourselves in the best position to achieve our goals. Having a healthy competitive spirit is part of the platform.

CHAPTER 7

DEFINITION VERSUS TRUE MEANING

I begin this chapter with a couple of questions for you and two quotes. I do so in taking a step to address the point that when some people encounter an obstacle or barrier in life, they see a problem. In fact, not only do they see a problem but the way they view the obstacle or barrier in their lives may just be the biggest problem of all for them.

Once we set a goal and set out on a mission to accomplish it, we are almost certain to encounter challenges along the way. The bigger the goal, the greater the probability of running into natural twists, turns, and roadblocks along the path to achieving it.

I will share more about what steps we can take to remain focused on our goals despite potential obstacles or barriers we may run into later. For now, our focus is on when a problem arises in our lives, how do we view the problem?

The first question I have for you is, "How do you respond when your expectations are not met?" You may want to jot down your answer to the question. Please take a moment and think about your answer to this question in preparation for the next one I have for you.

The second question is, "How do you respond when you run into an obstacle or barrier in your life?" Once again, you may want to write down your answer. Please take a moment and think about your answer to this question as well.

The first quote I would like to share with you is from Henry Ford. His vision and the Model T. Ford changed the way people traveled from home to work and to other places and back economically. His quote was:

"Most people spend more time and energy going around problems than in trying to solve them."

The second quote is from my mom. She was a single parent who raised 5 of her 11 children with the assistance of the welfare system. It was part of her mission to raise her children to be the best they could be. Her quote is:

"It's not a problem, as long as you can do something about it. The question is what are you going to do about it?"

My mom and Henry Ford are different in so many ways, yet they are alike in many ways. One of the ways they are very much alike is in the way they both thought. Especially when it comes to how they saw and responded to problems, as evidenced by their quotes.

One achieved his vision and mission by revolutionizing the automobile industry. The other raised her kids as a single parent to be the best they can be despite her difficult circumstances.

In a sense, the two of them represent the vast majority of the population on many fronts. They came from two different ends of the social and economic scale. Henry Ford was a billionaire; and my mom, well she raised her children on the welfare system.

Other ways in which they were very much alike is that both had a healthy competitive spirit and they were driven by a purposeful mission and vision in life. This showed in how they handled things when they encountered a problem in their lives. I've learned a great deal in my life from the both of them.

One of the things I learned from my mom revolves around values, life skills, and character traits. You see, when you think of words like courage, focus, faith, patience, persistence, determination, resiliency, forgiveness, commitment, healing, and others, these words have a definition; however, they have no true meaning in life until we have to apply them to the situation we're in. Often that is when we encounter obstacles or barriers in our lives.

When we ask someone the definition of one of these words, they can give us the answer. They can tell us the definition of courage, faith, persistence, resilience, and others. They can usually do the same when we inquire about the definition of knowledge and wisdom.

One of the aims of this book is to assist us in consistently bringing true meaning to these words in our lives when we need to apply them. Usually that's when we either run into a problem in life or when we encounter obstacles or barriers that can potentially hinder our ability to achieve our goals.

Another aim of this book is to assist us in bringing true meaning to the words knowledge and wisdom when we need to apply them to put ourselves in a position to achieve our goals in life. Once again, that's usually when we run into twists, turns, and roadblocks we naturally encounter along the path to achieving our goals in life.

Possessing these personal qualities is a part of the success patterns of highly effective people. That's the case whether you're a billionaire who revolutionized the automobile industry like Henry Ford or a single parent like my mom who raised her kids to be the best they could be while on the welfare system. These are the success patterns of people regardless of where they fall on the socio-economic scale.

People are often intrigued when they see good things happening in the lives of others who consistently practice solid success patterns. They admire the character traits possessed by these individuals.

Many people who are thus intrigued may be experiencing a situation they are seeking to change or avoid for themselves when they run into an obstacle or barrier in their lives and their immediate reaction may be to ask one of those individuals: "Teach me how you do what you do in your life." For some, they may be saying: "Provide me with some magic formula that will solve all my problems in my life."

These people may be seeking instant success in the attainment of their goals, or they may be asking for a quick fix to a problem they may have encountered along the path in pursuit of their goals. The success patterns we're learning in this book do not and will not provide instant success in the accomplishment of our goals, nor will they provide a quick fix to the problems we encounter.

As opposed to providing a quick fix, one of the book's objectives is for us to learn how to bring true meaning to those characteristics when we need to apply them, especially as we journey through the natural phases of transition and change in our lives. That's because there's no instant access to goal attainment just as there is no quick fix to many of the problems we face in life.

At World Class Coaches, we see and hear the quick fix approach often in the form of people sharing some of the following with us:

> *"My (husband or wife) never listens to me. I tell (him or her) what I want, but they never listen. Everything seems to always fall on my shoulders. I try to communicate this point to (him or her), but I can never get them to listen. I can't count on (him or her) for anything. If I don't do it myself, it won't get done; yet, I have all these things to do, and no one to help me do them."*

> *"I know I need to lose weight. I've tried several different diets, but none of them seem to be the right one for me. I set goals in this area of my life and things go well for*

me for a while, and then it just seems I lose steam and things fizzle out for me. I seem to have difficulty holding myself accountable."

"I have a desire to take my business to the next level, but I seem to be stuck. I've tried several different programs; however, they don't seem to work for me. In some cases, I even changed programs in an effort to find the right fit for me, but it just did not work out for me."

When you look at these statements, you get a sense that these people may be looking for the answers outside of themselves. They may be looking for a quick fix in the form of the next magic diet formula, motivational speech, or training program that will provide them with the answers. They may be looking for all the solutions outside of themselves when the answers may reside inside of them.

Again, when a problem arises, highly effective people first look to refocus on the target they are pursuing. In the midst of the challenges or setbacks they may be encountering they "lock on" to their desired outcome and "lock out" the chaos that may be contributing to the challenges they're facing.

With focus and their desired outcome in mind they look inside and ask themselves, "What can I do to resolve this problem?" They know this is the time when they will need to tap into their healthy competitive spirit and bring true meaning to words like having courage, faith, being patient, persistent, resilient, or other applicable character words, when they need to do so, based on the current situation they are facing at the moment. They do so to assist them in taking the next step toward the attainment of the goals they're pursuing despite certain circumstances they may be facing.

CHAPTER 8

NATURAL GROWTH PHASES

When parents welcome a new baby to the family, they usually begin the process of setting goals for their child the moment the baby is born. That's usually the case whether it's their first child or the addition of a new son or daughter to their family. They set goals that not only include the health and safety of their new baby but also ones that include them to become highly educated.

Furthermore, they set a goal to instill strong values and character traits in their kids. That includes teaching life skills that will enable their kids to become courageous, focused, patient, and resilient as they grow. They're looking to instill success patterns that will enable them to become successful in whatever space they choose in life.

Life is a continual process of transition and change, whether we're ready for it or not. Along the way, there are natural growth phases we all go through. One of them revolves around the learning process kids go through in our country's educational system. This is widely applicable and available to all and is used to assist parents in helping them achieve their goal of providing their kids with a high-quality education, including preparing them for college.

Many parents begin taking steps to achieve their goals for their children by reading to them regularly at a very young age. As they grow, they continue reading to them and may purchase additional educational resources and tools to further enhance their efforts in attaining the goal of their kids' becoming well educated.

For parents, as their children grow closer to kindergarten and elementary school age, their focus shifts. They begin looking for a desired school system to gain access to the kind of education they're seeking for their children once they start school.

They continue to take steps to make sure their kids are in the best school they can find as they transition through elementary, junior high or middle school, and ultimately through high school. They may even consider moving or relocating their family to a new neighborhood or city in search of what they believe to be a better school system.

The search often doesn't stop when their son or daughter graduates from high school. For those parents who can afford it or are expecting their child to win a scholarship, the search continues with helping them look for a college of their choice to attend. Other parents often search for a way to pay the cost of their children attending college or they may take out loans.

Although many parents begin educating their children early, they don't always coach them on instilling life skills and character traits that often assist in leading to the development of the success patterns of highly effective people. It's not because they don't desire to take this step and it's not because they are not great parents because they may be super parents. It's just that they may not have the type of experiential platform themselves to effectively teach these specific life skills and character traits shared in the following paragraph. Although they may be learned in other ways, their growth experiences generally occurred through their participation in extracurricular activities.

Participating in extracurricular activities provides real-time life experiences that teach kids to become courageous, focused, dedicated, persistent, and resilient individuals as they grow through the youth, teenage, and young adult years. It starts out when they're old enough to begin learning values and life skills and continues through a process of growth and development that will last a lifetime.

However, there certainly may be other ways to learn these skills. But the teaching and learning of these valuable skills and character traits are certainly one of the reasons why parents are encouraged to work with their children to become engaged in an extracurricular activity of their choice during their school age years.

As previously mentioned, children's participation in extracurricular activities provides them with a purposeful platform on which to build character and enhance life skills and values that they may find difficult to learn elsewhere. It can also assist them in developing new friendships on a safe platform, especially when they move or relocate to a new neighborhood or school.

These core tenets are some of the contributing factors to why young kids are encouraged to be involved with an extracurricular activity. We're not concerned about which activity as long as they're participating in an activity of their choice that they enjoy.

Another reason for getting young children involved in activities is because kids don't stay kids for very long. They're born, and through the natural process of growth and development they grow from a newborn, to an infant, to a toddler, and before you realize it they are preschool age. Then the next thing a parent realizes is that their precious child is now elementary school age.

It is at this point when parents begin the process of making decisions about which school system they will be choosing for their children's education. Once that decision is made, the children spend the next 12 years of their life growing and transitioning from elementary school, to middle school, and then ultimately to high school.

There are many challenges parents may face during these natural phases of their kid's school years. They could range from not having access to a desired school system for various reasons, or there could be the need for them to move or relocate their family because of a new job opportunity, or maybe even a job lost, or for still other reasons.

In addition to the challenges parents face, their children may face potential obstacles or barriers during these natural phases of transition and change in their lives. Many of them may be out of their control, such as what took place with me — the divorce of my parents.

Regardless of the circumstance, kids may be negatively affected by their situation, and this may present a potential threat to them in terms of using more of their full potential. This is especially true as they transition through the various phases of the school system.

This is important to remember because during all phases of life, there are incremental stages in the natural process of growth and development for each of us. That is certainly the case with kids going through the educational school system.

Think about this for a moment. Every year we have a new group of kids eligible to start preschool or elementary school for the very first time. And we have a new group of high school graduates and college graduates, all ready to transition to the next phase of their lives.

This also applies to them in the development of the success patterns of highly effective people. That includes them growing personally and professionally. They start as a newborn, and by the time they turn 17 or 18 they graduate from high school and are ready for college. After graduating from college, they're ready for everyday life.

Let's take a closer look at the transitions high school and college graduates go through. As students grow closer to graduating from high school, they are faced with having to make some critical decisions in their lives, whether they are ready to do so or not. The decisions revolve around what will the next phase of their life look like?

Many high school graduates may decide to continue their educational process by going to college. Others may decide to serve our country by joining the military. Others may decide to find a job and go to work at this time. And, there are a number of graduates who will find themselves in an uncertain future. That's because they are unclear where the next phase of their life is taking them.

One thing we know for certain is that many high school graduates will choose to continue their educational process by moving on to college if the opportunity presents itself. And, many parents desire their children to continue their educational process by going to college. The challenge is that many of the students feel that they may not be able to accomplish their goal of going to college for various reasons.

One of the main reasons why some people feel that college is out reach for their children is affordability and the costs of college tuition.

Although many parents may not be able to afford the cost of college tuition, the reality of the matter is that many high school graduates can put themselves in a position to go to college if they really desire to do so. If going to college is truly a part of their goals, then they are closer to achieving that goal than they may realize. First of all, they have already taken a giant step toward achieving that goal when they graduated from high school.

Another reason is that every year there are literally millions of dollars in financial aid, scholarships and grants available for students to use to attend college, some of which go unclaimed each year. The key here is if the high school graduate is truly committed to going to college, the question is: are they placing unnecessary limitations on themselves? Some people may be limiting themselves by the lens through which they see the problem or they may see other obstacles or barriers standing in the way of their achieving their goal of going to college.

If this is you, I encourage you to follow the advice of Henry Ford and my mom in their approach to dealing with problems.

If you recall Henry Ford's quote: "Most people spend more time and energy going around problems than in trying to solve them."

Henry Ford was a billionaire. What I encourage you to take away from his quote as it relates to this situation is to not spend your time and energy on the reasons why you cannot go to college; instead, spend it seeking to solve the problems standing in the way of your going to college.

If you recall, the quote from my mom was, "It's not a problem, as long as you can do something about it. The question is what are you going to do about it?"

My mom was a single parent who raised five of her 11 children with the assistance of the welfare system. She is saying, wait a minute, it's not a problem at all as long as you can do something about it. The question is what are you going to do about it?

Well, one of the things you can do about it is to take steps to identify and take advantage of the various financial aid, scholarships or grants that are available to qualifying candidates every year. By doing so, you move one step closer to achieving your goal of going to college to continue your education.

Now solving this problem will not be easy. In fact, it may very well be one of those journeys where you will need to bring the true meaning to character words like being courageous, focused, committed, persistent, and resilient as you search and pursue the scholarship opportunities.

For this reason, there a couple of other things I encourage you to take away from both quotes. And please remember, one is coming from a billionaire and the other is coming from a single parent on welfare. Despite their vast differences in status and economic wealth, they and everyone else in life encounter a wide array of problems in their lives. That includes individuals who feel they may not be able to attend college for whatever reason.

However, the main thing I encourage you to take away from this lesson is how they saw and sought to solve problems when they encountered them in life. In other words, both of their approaches are consistent with the success patterns of highly effective people.

One reason why this is important is that after a high school graduate begins his or her college career, there will come a time when they will become a college graduate and need to transition to everyday life. In other words, it will be decision-making time for them once they finish college, whether they're ready for it or not.

The decisions they will be faced with making during this chapter of their lives are similar to the ones everyone will face throughout their adult lives. These include where will they settle down and reside (which city or state) and what will they do for housing? Will they rent or purchase a home?

Another decision revolves around their need to identify the economic vehicle they will use in life to meet their financial needs or achieve their financial goals. Taking this step is usually referred to as finding a job to support yourself, or if you have a family, to support you and your family. You will read more about your economic vehicle later.

Taking these steps is not always easy for college graduates or anyone else. In fact, there are people of all ages and at various stages of their lives, who are simply wondering about the future throughout their lives because they are uncertain where the next phase of their life is taking them.

And it does not stop there at their graduation from college. As they continue through the next chapters of their lives they will have many more decisions to make about marriage, starting a family, and possible career changes. With each step taken, you move closer to achieving your overall mission, vision, purpose, and goals in life.

CHAPTER 9

PROBLEMS BRING STORMS IN LIFE

One of the things I learned from my mom came not necessarily from what she said, which was powerful, but from watching her. And specifically, from watching how she responded to things when her expectations were not met or when she encountered challenges or setbacks in her life. She was equally consistent in how she responded to things when her children ran into obstacles, barriers, or roadblocks or when we had setbacks in our lives.

Through my mom's parenting and by watching her practice what she was preaching to us on a daily basis, I learned a number of things. One of them is that as we go through life, from time-to-time and from phase-to-phase, we will encounter obstacles, barriers, and setbacks. We all will run into them regardless of who we are or where we fall on the socio-economic scale. Challenges equal problems, and problems bring about storms in our lives.

One of the most significant things I learned from my mom can best be described in the first sentence of her quote, "It's not a problem, as long as you can do something about it."

When you think about what she is actually saying here, she is saying, "Well, I don't know what kind of storm you've encountered in life, but there is one thing I do know. It's not a problem at all, as long as you can do something about it." She further validated her point by the question she asked to close out her statement, "The question is what are you going to do about it?".

She did so in an encouraging and inspiring manner by helping you see with her first sentence that the real question is when a storm rolls into your life, regardless of the size or its intensity, what are you going to do about it? While growing up as a kid, I learned a great deal from her because I saw her practice what she preached.

As you recall, words have a definition, but they have no true meaning until you apply them at the appropriate time and place in life. Well, I watched my mom time-and-time again bring true meaning to words like courage, patience, persistence, commitment, dedication, forgiveness, resiliency and others when she needed to apply them. She did so in the midst of storms in her life.

I also watched her take similar steps through the consistent manner in which she encouraged her children to apply these words when we needed to in our lives. It was through many of these experiences that I first began the process of learning the difference between a setback and a failure in your life, which we will talk more about later.

When you set a goal and begin to take steps to achieve it, there are going to be days when everything will go smoothly and as planned. This is definitely the case as you go through natural phases of transition and change in your life. However, there will be other days when you will run into twists, turns, and roadblocks during all stages of your life.

For example, let's take a deeper look at the high school students we previously talked about who recently graduated and set a goal to go to college. When the time came for them to take that step, reality set in with the thought that they might be unable to achieve their goal. That's because their families could not afford the college tuition. Therefore, the question is: Is this an obstacle, a barrier, or is it a setback or even a failure for the graduate? Either way, there's a problem, and that's lack of access to college tuition.

However, the question to the graduate is, what are you going to do about it?

When you think of possible solutions to the problem, we previously discussed taking steps to identify and apply to qualify for part of the millions of dollars of financial aid, scholarship and grant dollars that are available for college tuition each year. There are other students who are so committed to going to college and find themselves in a similar situation that they may take on one, maybe even two jobs to pay for the college tuition to put themselves through college. In both instances, the graduate is taking steps to resolve the problem, and by solving the problem, the lack of funding for college tuition becomes merely a temporary obstacle or barrier in life. Resolve the problem, and you're one step closer to achieving your goal whether you realize it or not at the moment.

CHAPTER 10

SETBACK VERSUS FAILURE

When I look back at my freshman year at the University of Texas, I recall getting off to a great start in football. I became a starter at the safety position almost the moment I set foot on campus. I played in our first three games of the season. However, in practice before our fourth game, I developed a deep thigh bruise. What was not thought to be a serious injury turned out to be one. It caused me to miss all of the remaining games on our schedule, with the exception of our team's final game my freshman year.

Although I missed all but four games that season, and as difficult and frustrating as it was to not be able to play a game I loved so much, the injury was merely a temporary setback in my life. I was able to resume my football career after the injury and go on to achieve my goal of playing for 10 years in the National Football League.

During that span, I had six other setbacks in the form of injuries during my football career. Each one caused me to miss playing time, and yes, they brought about storms in my life during that time. However, on each occasion, I was able to recover from them and continue on the path of attaining my goals in life.

As we journey through life, our lives may be filled with obstacles, barriers, and setbacks. These moments will primarily come in the form of adverse circumstances, some of which may be out of our control. These circumstances create storms in our lives. They often convey the need to bring true meaning to the character words when we need to apply them in order to put ourselves in a position to perform under pressure. How faithful we remain while in the midst of the storm will determine how well we remain focused on our goals.

As we travel through life, we will find that it is easy to remain faithful and focused on our goals when things are going well. However, one of the keys to putting ourselves in a position to achieve our goals is to remain focused and faithful in our ability to achieve them when we encounter storms in our lives.

This is an important reminder because we may never know the depth of our faith until we find ourselves in the midst of a storm. How we respond in that moment will provide us with a glimpse of who we see ourselves to be on the inside and the depth of our faith. This is when we get a preview of our subconscious beliefs.

When we find ourselves in the midst of a storm, our deep-seated beliefs and true character traits rise to the surface. This is when we learn whether we believe in who we say we are as a person or whether we are pretending to be someone or something on the outside that we are not on the inside.

We all encounter storms while pursuing our goals and dreams in life. How well we find our way around, over or through the rocks in the road when we encounter them will determine to what degree we realize our mission, vision, purpose, and goals in life.

Regardless of who we are, where we come from, what socio-economic level we fall in, or our chosen field or profession, we all encounter storms in our lives or rocks in the road that can get in the way of us achieving our goals in life. The key is how effectively we deal with them when we encounter them.

In other words, we all encounter storms in our lives or obstacles or barriers in the road as we journey through life. For some of us, the obstacles may be the size of a pebble. For others they are the size of a boulder, and for still others, these challenges are the size of mountains. Regardless of the size, the question is, what are we going to do about it?

One of the critical points we're encouraged to take away from this chapter is to understand the difference between a setback and a failure. This includes understanding the difference between what it means to fail at something and to label ourselves a failure.

When problems arise in our lives, storms usually follow. The thing to remember is that neither the problems nor the storms are equal to us being a failure in life. Sure enough, we may fail when taking certain steps or even fail to make the desired progress we envisioned making while pursuing our goals. However it's important to remember that "It's not a problem, as long as we can do something about it. The question is what we are going to do about it?"

That's never been more evident to me than my experience in the NFL as a pro football player. When we arrived at training camp each year, we knew that there was a probability that we might lose 25% to 40% of our games during the upcoming season but still have a chance to achieve our goal of winning the Super Bowl. In other words, we knew there would be some days and games that were not going to go our way. The question was what were we going to do about it when the storms rolled in?

One step was to make sure that we realized that a loss, or even a losing streak, did not equal failure. The losses or the losing streak may have been a temporary setback as it related to our goal; however, it did not equal being a failure as a team to us. That is basically the difference between a setback and a failure. But this approach can also lead to questions about everything from what is the problem to what is the solution to the problem when storms arrive?

No matter how we look at it, when challenges emerge, it's clear that we have a problem in our lives if the challenges are hindering our path to the achievement of our goals.

As we previously discussed, one of the challenges we face in this area of our lives is how we see the problem. In some cases, the way we see the problem may be the biggest problem of all because it relates to our ability to solve it.

Regardless of how we may view the problem, if we're interested in solving it we must find a solution. As we pursue the resolution to the problems standing between us and our goals, one of the things we must be aware of is that there are no "right or wrong" answers to many of the problems facing us. Oh sure, I understand that the answer to the math problem of $2 + 2 = 4$. We know this. But what we don't always know is the correct way to resolve many of the problems that may be causing the storms in our lives. Therefore, our aim is not to necessarily focus on one specific strategy.

Instead, our focus should be on improving the quality of the search for the potential resolution for the storms in our lives. Specifically, the solution lies in searching for meaningful ways to bring true meaning to the character words necessary to put us in a position to achieve our goals when we need to apply them.

In taking these steps, please remember that the problem with the "right answer" is that one person's "right answer" may be meaningless to someone else. When we look back with hindsight, time often reveals that a better way already existed but we just could not see it at the time. The best we can do is be humble, realizing that our existing way could always be better. Therefore, we should constantly be on a search for that better way to deal with the storms in our lives without losing sight of our aims in life. In doing so, we move one step closer to achieving our goals in life.

Start Where You Are	Success Habit Patterns	Driven by a Higher Purpose				

3

SECTION

DRIVEN BY A HIGHER PURPOSE

Goal attainment is a process driven by a higher purpose. While pursuing our purpose in life, we achieve our goals, one step at a time. Often, it requires us to have a purpose-driven platform and the focus and direction that will enable us to take the first step, then the next step, and the next, one at time, in pursuit of our higher purpose.

In this section, we will take steps to properly align our mission, vision, and goals with our purpose in life.

CHAPTER 11

WHAT'S DRIVING YOU IN LIFE?

By nature, as human beings we are goal-oriented. We operate better when we have goals in life that are driven by a higher purpose.

As human beings, we need a clear picture or target to move toward in life. We need a purpose and a vision. Without these targets, what basis would we use to make daily decisions in life?

One day while working in my office, I noticed that each of the three different clocks in the office indicated a different time of the day. Knowing that there's one correct time adjusted for the time zone we live in, I reflected for a moment on what makes each clock tick. I was interested in knowing why each one displayed a different time.

As I contemplated on what was possibly causing the difference in time, I focused on the power source for each clock. I noticed that two of the three clocks were powered by batteries only, while the third one received its power from an electrical power source. Although each showed a different time, each had some source of power.

While assessing the power source of each clock, I thought of a fourth clock—one which I relied on heavily—the one associated with my cell phone. Although powered by a battery, my cell phone clock had always proved to be very reliable. When I compared its time with that of the other three clocks, I noted that it had the same time as the clock powered by an electrical power source. I determined that these two clocks had the correct time.

What was curious to me was that the two clocks that showed the incorrect time were powered by batteries. Whether it was the age of the batteries or some other reason, something had affected what made those clocks perform properly.

I find these clocks to be apt metaphors for how we operate as human beings. As with the clocks, some power source affects our ability to be the best we can be.

For each of us, there is something or someone guiding or directing us in life. Right now, you may be driven by a circumstance or problem in your life. Or you may be driven by fears from your past.

There are hundreds of circumstances, conditions, or emotions that drive our lives. Some are positive and others are negative. The following are six power sources that are usually negative:

1. **Fear.** Some people are driven by fear. Often, this is the result of growing up with unrealistic expectations, a failed marriage, or a failed business experience. Fear-driven people often miss out on opportunities because of their fears. Fear prevents them from utilizing more of their God-given potential and realizing more of their goals.

2. **Anger.** Some people are driven by resentment and anger. They experience hurt or pain as a result of others or circumstances and they hold on to them instead of releasing them through forgiveness. Some resentment-driven people "clam up" and internalize their anger, while others "blow up" and

explode their anger onto others. Both can affect our ability to utilize more of our potential and bring true meaning to character words when we need to apply them.

3. **Guilt.** Some people are driven by guilt. They allow their past to control their future. They often punish themselves by sabotaging their own success. They spend their time running from regrets. People who live with guilt often find themselves wandering through life without a sense of direction or purpose.

4. **Need for Approval.** Some people are driven by the need for approval from others. For example, some may go through life seeking the approval from their parents. Others allow the expectations of their spouse, children, friends, coworkers, or peer pressure to control their lives. They're worried about what someone else may say or think about them. Being controlled by the opinions of others can greatly contribute to our failure to utilize more of our God-given potential and prevent us from achieving more of our goals.

5. **The Need to Please.** Some people are driven by the need to please others. They have a need to be all things to all people. They are controlled by the inability to say no! They often find themselves spread so thin that they have difficulty focusing on any one thing long enough to complete the task. Being controlled by the need to please others is a sure way to find yourself traveling through life with a lot of undue pressure and unnecessary stress.

6. **Possessions**. Some people are driven by material possessions. They think the more things they have, the happier or more important they'll be. They are driven by a label or a title. They have the feeling that their status will bring them more security,

self-fulfillment, and peace. That's not the case! Material possessions are temporary. They can be lost instantly through a variety of uncontrollable circumstances.

ONE SURE POWER SOURCE

There is one sure power source to keep us focused on our goals.

7. *Purpose*. Many people are driven by a purpose in life. Knowing our purpose gives us meaning in life. It provides us with focus, drive, and motivation. Having a purpose provides us with a mission in life; it is what makes us tick. It becomes the standard we use to determine which activities are essential to assisting us in fulfilling our mission, vision, and goals in life. It's the foundation on which we build and decide where we spend our time and how we use our resources. It's the power source that drives us in life.

People who live their lives without a clear purpose and mission usually try to be all things to all people. They tend to go through life making decisions based on the circumstances of others or comments they hear from other people. Often, they try to take on more than they can handle at the time, which leads to a life full of conflicts. That's because without a purpose in life, we have no foundation by which to make effective decisions regarding where we spend our time and how we utilize our resources.

These people go through life without direction and focus. They are looking for security in all the wrong places; they are driven by factors outside of them. This often leads to frustration after frustration and living an unfulfilled life. Figuring out what makes you tick in life can lead to your being one step closer to achieving your overall mission, vision, purpose, and goals in life.

CHAPTER 12

LIVE A PURPOSE-DRIVEN LIFE

When I think of my mom, I often think of her comments, "I was placed here to raise my kids to be the best that they can be. That is my purpose in life. That's why God put me here."

When I think of Henry Ford and his purpose with Ford Motor Company, I think of how he revolutionized the automobile industry.

When you study highly effective people, regardless of their chosen field or profession, one thing you notice about them is that they appear to be driven by a higher purpose, supported by their mission, vision, and goals in life. Many feel they have a compelling reason to be here on earth — a purpose in life. They pursue their mission, vision, purpose, and goals with love and passion. That's what drives them.

In observing highly effective people, you notice that their purpose in life usually involves serving, helping, or entertaining others. They create an economic vehicle or identify a way to serve or help others in need to the best of their abilities. And they manage to stay true to their purpose, even during storms in their lives.

The better they are at helping others meet their needs or achieving their goals, the more special blessings appear to flow their way.

If you're among the people who are living your life without focus or direction, I encourage you to ask yourself the question, "Why am I here on earth?" It appears that many billionaires and other highly effective people have asked themselves that question, and their answer led them to serving, meeting the needs of, or entertaining millions, even billions of people around the world.

Many highly effective people acquire a great deal of wealth, and they deserve it; however, it is not necessarily the money that they are pursuing. It's the realization of their mission, vision, and goals, driven by their purpose in life. That's what drives them. With this approach, financial rewards appear to flow their way.

In fact, when you observe highly effective people such as founders of publicly held companies, professional athletes, entertainers, elite sales professionals, and others, one of the things you notice about them is that they are among the highest paid people in their chosen fields. The better they are at bringing their mission, vision, and purpose to light, the more they are compensated. With this approach, financial rewards are abundant.

This group of highly effective people represent a certain portion of the population who have identified their purpose in life and clearly aligned their mission, vision, and goals with their purpose. They have identified an economic vehicle and developed the skills in their chosen field to bring their mission, vision, purpose, and goals to life. For them, being the best they can be despite their circumstances is part of what drives them.

The question is what enables highly effective people to remain focused on their goals, while others may easily be knocked off theirs? Part of the answer can be found in their ability to live a purpose-driven life.

If you have not already done so, I encourage you to ask yourself the question, "Why am I here on earth?" In answering the question, you will begin the process of identifying your purpose in life.

CHAPTER 13

ALIGN YOUR VISION WITH YOUR PURPOSE

When I arrived in the NFL with the Los Angeles Rams, I set a goal to play for 10 years in the league. During my seventh year, I had a vision. I envisioned the coaching process that we use so successfully as professional athletes against the world's greatest competition in the most hostile environments being available to all sectors of society. I shared my vision with my life coach, who asked how large I wanted my playing field to be. Did I want it to be just in Los Angeles, or did I want it to be something larger? I told him that I did not know. Well, he told me to think about it, and I agreed to do so.

I loved playing football. It was something I was passionate about. However, I wanted more out of life than to just be known as a football player. One of my fears during my professional football career was not knowing if I would ever find something to replace playing football with in my life after retirement. What I was most concerned about was finding something that I could pursue with the same love and passion with which I pursued sports.

Well, six months after my life coach asked me to think about how large I would like my playing field to be, I arrived at a decision. I told him that I would like it to be the world. And from that vision, World Class Coaches, the international personal, professional, and executive coaching company I lead today was born. With that, my vision of making the coaching process we use as professional athletes available to all sectors of society became a reality. The company coaches across all industry lines.

As a professional athlete, I was accustomed to taking steps daily to put myself in the best position for success — to be the best I could be despite circumstances. The purpose of the coaching process and the steps taken daily are all designed to accomplish this goal.

It was during this time that my true purpose in life started to become crystal clear to me. God put me here on the face of this earth and blessed me with the gifts and talents He provided me with the gift to "Empower people to use more of their God-given potential despite circumstances." He put me here to help people be the best they can be, especially during periods of transition and change in their lives.

The World Class Coaches' mission is driven by five words: "Serve – Protect – Inspire – Encourage – Empower." The company's mission is to empower individuals to achieve more of their God-given potential and significantly increase their performance capability despite any adverse circumstances.

The company is committed to assisting our customers and clients in meeting their needs and achieving their goals with peace. Our commitment is to inspire, encourage, and empower our customers and our client's entire family to be the best they can be throughout their lifetimes, specifically during periods of transition and change in their lives. A specific focus is placed on the protection of their children during periods of transition and change in their lives. Our commitment extends to the children's grandparents, aunts, uncles, and cousins.

The vision for World Class Coaches is to be dominant worldwide in empowering individuals to achieve more of their God-given potential and significantly increase their performance capability.

There is no doubt that my mom's mission and purpose in life and my long professional sports career laid a foundation for my purpose in life. Although they were on two totally different ends of the spectrum, the focus of both revolved around using our full potential and being the very best we can be despite our circumstances in life.

There's no doubt that my life coach's inquiry of how large I wanted my playing field to be played a key role in my clarifying my purpose and mission in life. My coach assisted me in properly aligning my vision with my purpose and mission.

One thing became crystal clear to me as I was taking steps to clarify and properly align my vision with my purpose in life. We are often closer than we think to achieving our goals whether we realize it or not. And frequently a simple question, "How large would you like your playing field to be?" may be all we need to encourage us to take the next step in moving closer to the attainment of our goals. This is an example of what coaching consists of in the NFL, and it's an example of what it looks like in all sectors of society.

One thing I've become more aware of from my experience in coaching and training thousands of individuals is that those who have a clear purpose and vision approach life with more love and passion. They seem to consistently be on a mission in life. Those who lack a clear vision aligned with their purpose sometimes struggle with a lack of meaning and direction. Some even feel like a failure.

I learned many things from elite coaches in the sports world. One of them is that they have a unique ability to take a group of individuals from different backgrounds and all walks of life, bring them together, and create a powerful team vision and mission driven by a higher purpose.

They do so with people from different backgrounds, different beliefs, habits, and attitudes; some are people with huge egos and personalities who are paid millions of dollars for their athletic talents. Somehow, they are able to keep the team focused on their goals and vision when things are not going as planned for them or despite negative comments they hear from others that are not aligned with their vision, mission, or goals. If you were to ask them what's their purpose in life? Many of them will say, "Getting the most out of the people they coach." That is what drives them.

Therefore, I encourage you to answer the following questions as they relate to where you are at present in your life today. Please answer them in writing.

- Why are you here on earth?
- What drives you in life?
- What makes you tick in life?
- What is your mission in life?
- What is your purpose in life?
- What is your vision in life?

If you own a business or are interested in starting one, please answer the following questions:

- How large would you like your playing field to be?

We should think seriously about these questions because the answers are critical to our future. Our vision, mission, and purpose in life are the guiding forces behind the goals we set for ourselves. They give meaning to our existence.

Having a crystal-clear vision that is properly aligned with our purpose is an important part of creating direction and motivation for us in our lives. It provides a target for us to aim for in order to fulfill our purpose.

Without a purpose and vision, we may tend to drift through life and be controlled by external drivers, ranging from fear to resentment, anger, material possessions, the need to please others, or some other influence. With a clearly defined purpose, we're better able to make choices and decisions that support our vision in life.

For many of us, living life without a vision and goals leads to chaos and frustration. If we fail to establish these, we have no basis for making effective daily decisions.

Our purpose in life is like the rudder on a ship – it provides us with direction in life. It ensures that the results we're seeking are aligned with our vision. It helps us determine our priorities in life. Our mission ensures that we take the right steps to arrive at our intended destination and that the journey is just as important as achieving the goal.

We all need goals to move toward — a target to aim for in life. As human beings, we are built to have something pulling at us from the future. We seem to thrive when we have direction in life, something we are striving for, a mission and purpose in life. We can develop a sense of hopelessness when we lose that sense of direction. We do so because there's nothing really important to us. If we're going to live life to the fullest and find that inner peace, self-satisfaction, and self-fulfillment we desire in life, we not only need goals and a mission but we also need meaning and a purpose.

In other words, setting and achieving goals that simply enable us to own more things won't bring us lasting happiness and inner peace. Of course, financial success is important, but if the only reason we're working is so we can buy a new car every year or live in a fancy house that we fill with expensive furniture, we probably won't feel fulfilled. We'll never be able to buy enough or have enough. We'll keep raising the bar, having to own more and more, and we'll still feel that something is missing in our lives.

So it's important for us to know our purpose in life and to believe strongly in what we're pursuing in life. We should ask ourselves why we want to succeed, why we chose our goals, why we do the work we do, and what is really important to us. It's important to ask ourselves what's really driving us.

It's also important to remember that the ultimate goals we are striving to achieve must be properly aligned with the process we're using to achieve them. If we believe our family is important in our lives but our job or career goals are keeping us too busy to spend much time with them, something is out of alignment. If our mission in life is to make the world a better place, but we can't find time to support a good cause in our community, something is also wrong.

It's important for us to set our goals so that they support and advance our purpose and mission in life. This includes identifying all the key areas of our lives and aiming for balance. It's important that we make sure we set goals in all the key areas that are important to us. There's always time for the important things because we're the ones making decisions regarding where we spend our time in life.

As long as we're aware of our priorities, have a clear purpose in life, and say no to those things that conflict with our mission, vision, purpose, and goals, we can make solid daily decisions that will enable us to remain focused on our aims in life despite interfering circumstances.

CHAPTER 14

ALIGN VISION, MISSION, PURPOSE, AND VALUES

There are many different twists, turns, or roadblocks we encounter as we transition through life. Many of them can hinder our ability to achieve our goals. There's no greater obstacle than when we have a conflict with our values in life.

Values reflect the principles that are important to a family, society, entity, or to an individual. In business, stated values serve as guidelines for making policy and other decisions and for setting priorities. For individuals, they serve as criteria for making decisions that often become life changing. Values define the character and personality of the entity or the individual.

Values are more fundamental than vision and mission statements. In entities, values are often the real reasons a business is in existence. For individuals, values can be the basis for making life or death decisions. They certainly provide a basis for making many fundamental decisions (for example, spouse selection, career selection). Understanding values is very important and essential to analyzing the causes of human action or inaction.

There are many good values and selecting the few that are most important requires a lot of self-analysis, whether they are for a business, family, or an individual.

In business, values are selected by the owners or the management and certainly by the leadership. The process of identifying the business values to emphasize is an opportunity to elicit positive responses from various audiences.

Obviously, there are many values that are required for success in any field. By selecting certain values, for example in a value statement, an opportunity is provided to create a culture that has the characteristics that the management or owners believe will lead to success in the field of competition (for shareholders, for customers, for employees, for partners, and for suppliers.)

Values provide constraints on our mission, vision, purpose, and goals. They are the underlying fuel that drives the entity or the individual. This is why it's vitally important to make sure our mission, vision, purpose, and goals are properly aligned with our values, whether we're an entity, business, family, or individual.

At each level of my sports career, the head football coach began the season by addressing the entire team and laying out the expectations for the team. They covered the team's mission, vision, and goals, which were put in writing and reviewed daily.

This process assisted in the alignment of the team goals with its mission and vision. Proper alignment and clarity are two of the keys to establishing focus and direction. Creating and putting our mission, vision, purpose, goals, and value statements in writing and reviewing them daily assisted us in creating clarity. Proper alignment of our statements will assist us in creating more direction in our lives.

When writing our mission statement, it should describe our main purpose as an individual or entity. For an individual it should describe our purpose in life stated in terms of why God placed us here as an individual and the contribution we can make to ourselves, our family, or to society. For an entity, we should be a description of their chosen charter, stated in terms of their contribution to their customers or the market.

For an individual, the mission statement provides a sense of purpose and all the benefits that derive from having such a sense of purpose. These include a higher sense of self-esteem, motivation, direction, and well-being.

For an entity, the mission statement should be broad enough to include all the activities in which the entity wishes to engage. It should be narrow enough to eliminate activities that do not fit the charter. The charter is useful for keeping the entity focused on its main business while avoiding the pursuit of opportunities that are not properly aligned with the vision, purpose, and goals of the business.

In general, our business or entity's mission statement should be short, memorable, and easy to describe. It's our answer to the question "What drives you?" For an entity, it's the answer that employees should be able to give in 30 seconds or less when asked: "What does our company do?"

Every word in our mission statement should be carefully selected to accurately describe our purpose. If our mission statement is too long, complicated, or hard to describe, it can lead to a lack of clarity.

Conversely, a mission statement that is easily understood is easier to ingrain in others and will create a faster response, improved decision-making, better judgment, priority-setting, and concerted power in the activities you take on.

In writing your vision statement, keep in mind that it is a word picture of success for an individual or for an entity. It's a brief description of the desired outcome we're pursuing, which we can easily visualize and comprehend. Our vision is the end result we're seeking when our mission is being accomplished. It is the picture for success toward which our goals are directed.

In writing your vision statement, describe your personal vision in life without placing any limitations on yourself. Often we set goals based on our perceived available resources to achieve them.

Begin by asking the question, "If resources were not a factor, what would my life look like? What would it look like in 5 years, in 10 years, and beyond?"

In answering these questions, describe those things you have always wanted to do but for various reasons you have not done thus far. Utilize your answers as a part of describing your vision. In a precise manner, describe what you really want in life.

If your mission does not support the attainment of your vision, and purpose, one or the other needs to be adjusted. If your goals and action plans are not leading you toward making the vision a reality, then your plans may not be focused on accomplishing the right mission. When you properly align your mission, vision, purpose, and goals with your values in writing and review them daily, you take steps to move closer to achieving your aims in life.

SECTION 4

CLARIFY YOUR CURRENT REALITY

Goal attainment is a process driven by a higher purpose. In pursuit of our purpose in life, we achieve our goals one step at a time. Often it requires us to have a purpose-driven platform and the focus and direction that will enable us to take the first step, then the next step, one at a time, to put ourselves in a position to achieve our aims despite certain circumstances. This can sometimes be a challenge for many of us because we lack clarity in terms of where we stand today in our current reality. In this section, we will clearly determine where we stand today in our current reality as it relates to our mission, vision, purpose, goals, and values.

CHAPTER 15

BEGIN WITH WHERE YOU ARE TODAY IN CURRENT REALITY

One of the most valuable resource tools available today to assist us in efficiently navigating directions is our GPS system. The purpose of this tool is to efficiently guide us by means of a navigation process from our current location to a predetermined desired location successfully. It requires us to know our end result and then take one step to program the system to navigate directions. Once we take that step, the tool has been programmed to guide us to our desired destination.

So, when was the last time you used your GPS system? For many of us, it was recently. Regardless, of when we last used it, when we did we took an essential step — we programmed in our chosen destination.

As great a resource as our GPS is, it requires us to know the address or landmark where we desire to be at the end of our trip. With this knowledge, we are required to take a step moving us toward the attainment of our goal -- plugging in our final destination.

Once we have taken that step, the GPS navigating system goes to work. It has been preprogrammed to determine where we're presently located. Not only has it been programmed to figure out our current location but once we plug in our destination, the navigating system will begin providing directions to guide us to our desired end location. Once we begin driving, the navigation system will continue to provide us with directions even if we make a wrong turn or take a detour. In this instance, it will automatically adjust to guide us to our destination. The system has been programmed to take these steps.

Often, when we are driving to a desired location, and we're not certain how to get there, we feel challenged and frustrated. That's definitely the case when traveling without our navigation system. Our GPS system has been programmed to assist us in removing some of the chaos and frustration from our lives when we are seeking to travel efficiently and safely from where we are at present to a desired location.

Just as seeking to drive to a desired destination without our GPS navigation system can be challenging and frustrating, trying to travel through life without a designated target to aim for and a game plan to get us there can be equally as challenging and frustrating. This is especially true as we journey through the various natural phases of life that we all travel through during our lifetimes. To better understand this logic, let's take a closer look at why and how our GPS navigating system works so effectively.

First, as previously mentioned, our GPS requires us to know and plug in our desired destination. Once we have taken that step, the GPS navigating system goes to work. It has been preprogrammed to determine our present location. That is a critical step. That's because the navigating system will use it to make decisions on what route to take to guide us to our desired location.

Therefore, our GPS navigating system needs us to take certain steps to prepare it to guide us from our current location to our desired destination. The same thing must take place during the process of goal setting and goal attainment in our lives. We must clearly identify and properly align our mission with our purpose and then align our vision, mission, goals, and purpose in life with our values in order to establish our aims in life. Then we will need to take one additional critical step to program our internal GPS navigating system for everyday life. We must clearly establish where you are today in "Current Reality" in relation to our aims in life. In taking these steps, we create a gap in our lives between our objectives in life and where we are today in "Current Reality."

Occasionally, when some of us establish a vision and set goals, we leave out an important part of the process. We fail to clearly determine where we stand today in "Current Reality" relative to the targets we're pursuing. We fail to create a gap in our lives. This is an important step because it can affect many of the decisions we make as we transition through life and take steps to achieve our goals.

To begin creating a gap in our lives, we take our goals we wrote down: the purpose driving our mission and our vision and values from the previous section. Next, we clearly identify where we are today in "Current Reality" in relation to our aims, thereby formulating the gap. This is a step we definitely want to take in writing.

We can begin by describing those things we have become accustomed to in life both personally and professionally. In addition, we want to describe our personal and professional life today, including if we're single or married, where we work, where we stand financially, the beliefs, habits, and attitudes we possess, our skills, and last, our strengths and weaknesses. When we take this step, we're describing our lives today as we see them through our eyes in "Current Reality."

Once we've taken these steps to create the gap, understanding the role it plays in our lives is an integral measure to taking steps to achieve our goals and realizing more of our mission, vision, and purpose. Once we create the gap between our aims and the current reality in our lives, we take a giant step toward creating more focus and direction in our lives. We create an "Area of focus" in our lives.

THE GAP TECHNIQUE™

MISSION

VISION
PURPOSE
GOALS
VALUES

ECONOMIC VEHICLE

CURRENT REALITY

By seeing the gap between our current reality and our long-term target, we can better determine what steps are necessary to achieve our goals and realize our mission, vision, and purpose in life.

By the way, here's a reminder. Once we define a gap in our lives and take steps to close it, we never really actually close the gap, even though we may be achieving our goals. Once we start to achieve our goals and close in on our vision, everything moves up. That's because goal setting is an ongoing process.

For example, when I was in college I set a goal not just to make it to the National Football League but to play for 10 years once I arrived there. Once I was drafted into the League, my focus shifted to practicing the success patterns of highly effective professional football players, specifically the ones who had played for 8, 10, or 12 years in the League.

If we find ourselves without a gap or if we allow ourselves to close one without creating another one, we may lose our drive and motivation. One contributing element to our energy and drive involves the desire to close the gap between our mission, vision, and current reality. As human beings, part of our drive and motivation come from having clearly defined lifetime goals in order to assist us in closing the gap.

The next time and every time you use your GPS navigating system to get to your desired destination, I encourage you to think about the gap in your life.

By having a rock-solid starting point and a precise destination to shoot for in life in the form of our short or long-term aims, we're able to establish a precise game plan to close the gap. This game plan is guided by a clearly-defined, purposeful mission and supported by solid values. When properly aligned, our mission, vision, purpose, and values provide a rock-solid foundation to assist us in remaining focused on our goals, even when we find ourselves in a storm. By taking these steps, we move closer to achieving our goals in life.

CHAPTER 16

THE POWER OF A PURPOSEFUL ECONOMIC VEHICLE

Many of us as adults own an automobile. The vast majority of us use our vehicle for one primary purpose: to get from point "A to point B" in our lives. We use our GPS navigating system to direct and guide us, and we use our automobile to get us from one place to another – to our desired destination. Combined, the two make for an excellent platform to get us from a current location to a desired one by car.

Once we establish a gap in our lives, certain things need to take place for us to close the gap. Goal attainment is a process driven by a higher purpose. In pursuit of our purpose, we achieve our goals, one step at a time. Often, this process requires us to have a purpose-driven platform and the focus and direction that will enable us to take the first step, then the next step, one at time, to put us in the best position to achieve our overall goals in spite of certain negative circumstances.

One of the critical elements of a purpose-driven platform is the economic vehicle we select to assist us in getting from where we are today in current reality to our desired outcomes — the attainment of our aims in life. This vehicle is designed to be used for a purpose similar to that of our automobile as it relates to getting us from point A to point B. The core components of a sound economic vehicle in life are to assist us in:

- Meeting the specific needs of the consumers we serve,
- Supporting and protecting our family,
- Meeting our financial needs,
- Achieving our financial goals,
- Realizing our mission, vision, goals, and purpose.

One of the steps we take at World Class Coaches is to consistently remind athletes participating in high school, college, and especially those in professional sports, both male and female, that playing a professional sport is not their economic vehicle. That's the case, even though you hear about professional athletes receiving huge multimillion-dollar contracts.

In other words, during my NFL career I realized that playing pro football was not my economic vehicle in life. It was not something I would be able to do for the rest of my life no matter how much I loved the game. Playing the sport did not provide me the core components of a sound and lasting economic vehicle. However, playing the sport did provide me with a great stepping stone for the next phase of my life.

One of the things I became keenly aware of during my playing days in the NFL was that the billionaire owners had a powerful and purposeful economic vehicle that they could use for a life time and it was not necessarily the team that they owned. It was their private business or businesses that they owned. These assets provided them with the core components of a sound economic vehicle in whatever space they operated. In certain cases, it was the success of that economic vehicle that enabled them to realize a part of their overall vision of owning an NFL team.

Something else was evident in my life, and that was the difficulties professional athletes face when they transition from their playing days to everyday life. For many, it's hard leaving behind a game they love so dearly.

What makes it even more challenging is when the former players have difficulty finding an economic vehicle which they can pursue with all the same love and passion with which they pursued the game they left behind, one that contains all the core components of a sound economic vehicle, including enabling them to support and protect their families, meet their financial needs, and achieve their financial goals. They need one that will enable them to realize more of their personal and professional mission, vision, goals, and purpose in life. Often the former player's inability to take these steps and create a new economic vehicle contributes significantly to his or her inability to have a successful transition to the next phase of life.

There is something else I've become aware of through my work at World Class Coaches. The difficulty in transitioning is not something that just professional athletes face when they move to the next phase of their lives. When students head off to college and consider what they're going to study or major in or what career or profession they would like to pursue, they are preparing for the day they will be searching for the right economic vehicle for them, one with all the core components of a sound economic vehicle.

The same can be said about any of us going through one of the natural phases of transition and change we go through at different times in our lives. This is particularly the case when we look for work, seek a new job opportunity, or look to change careers or professions as part of the process.

Bottom line: what the student, former professional athlete, or a person in any space is looking for when they're looking for work is a career change that is a powerful and sound economic vehicle to get them from point A to point B in their life, one that will assist them in closing the gap between where they are today in current reality and their mission, vision, purpose, and goals. This change will enable them to feel inner peace, self-fulfillment, and self-satisfaction in life.

Ultimately, the purpose of our economic vehicle is to get us to a place where we have freedom of choice as to where and how we spend our time purposefully. Therefore, our economic vehicle in life is much more than a degree in our chosen field, or a job, a profession, an occupation, or owning our own business. However, having a degree in our chosen field surely enhances our probability of success. It's even more so because it equips us with the necessary core elements to consistently meet the specific needs of the consumers we serve in our chosen field or profession. It also enables us to earn the income or revenue necessary to support and protect our family. It's a vehicle to enable us to meet our financial needs, achieve our financial goals, and live the life style we desire as we naturally transition through the various stages of our lives.

For many highly effective people, their purpose in life involves serving, helping, or entertaining others. They create or identify an economic vehicle to serve or help others in need or to entertain others to the best of their abilities, and they stay true to their purpose even during storms in their lives. The better they become at helping others meet their needs or achieve their goals, the more special blessings appear to flow their way.

CHAPTER 17

CLOSING THE GAP IN LIFE IS HARD WORK

I begin this chapter by simply saying that life can be tough at times. Regardless of the contributing factors or who we are, there are times when it's difficult to make progress.

I will also share that some of us set up goals and then expect immediate success in their attainment. There may be instances in which we may experience that type of success; however, the bigger the goal, the tougher it will be to accomplish. The bigger the goal, the chances of running into roadblocks or having setbacks during the journey to goal attainment increase dramatically.

There are occasions when after we work through the various obstacles or barriers in life to ultimately achieve our goal, it can sometimes seem like the success came fast and out of nowhere. At least that's how it may seem to others; however, those of us who worked hard to accomplish the goal know that is definitely not the case.

I remember taking a trip back to my home town of La Grange shortly after being drafted by the Los Angeles Rams into the NFL.

During my visit, I had an opportunity to visit with a number of my former high school teammates. We reminisced about our high school days, including rejoicing in the glory of winning the state high school football championship during our high school career. During the conversation, one of my former teammates said to me, "Johnnie, when you were in high school, I knew you were good in football, but I never thought you were an All-American, and #1 draft pick in the NFL. And I can't believe how fast you got there."

That's when I said to him, "Wait a minute, what do you mean how fast I got there? Do you know how long and hard I had to work to become an NFL player? I began playing football in the 7th grade. I went on to play two years of junior high, four years of high school, and then four years of college football in preparation for accomplishing my goal of playing in the NFL.

"I spent the past 10 years of my life working diligently at being the best I could be each and every day and season after season for each year I played the sport. I spent many days over the past 10 years going to school, working out in the weight room, practicing on the field, and playing football games; I did that year after year, all preparing for the NFL. For you, it may have seemed like I got there really fast; however, to me, it took every single day of that 10-year period for me to ultimately achieve my goal of play-ing in the NFL."

When I look back on things, I realize that I was actually one step closer to achieving my goal of playing in the NFL when I signed up to play football in the 7th grade and every year there-after; however, I just didn't realize it at the time. I understand that not every player who sets a goal to play in the NFL as a young teenager will eventually play pro football. I also understand that not every person who sets a goal to attend college will ultimately achieve that goal. However, if both are to be realized, it's not going to happen overnight, and there will be a lot of hard work along the way. It's the hard work that we have to prepare for.

As we covered earlier, often when parents welcome a newborn baby to their family they set a goal for them to get a high-quality education and to instill certain character traits, life skills, and values in their child almost the moment he or she is born. Some of their goals is for their son or daughter to grow up to be the most courageous, patient, persistent, determined, and resilient person he or she can be.

Parents who are committed to consistently taking steps to instill these character traits in their children are wise in their thinking. That's because closing the gap in our lives is really hard work. Therefore being strong in our faith and being equipped with the success patterns of highly effective individuals will be advantageous when things become hard for us in life. We must surround our strength with the life skills, character traits, and values we possess.

Through the coaching process at World Class Coaches, we've discovered three primary contributing factors to why closing the gap in our lives can be so difficult. They appear in the form of:

- Circumstances we find ourselves in;

- Things not going as planned in our lives;

- Negative comments we hear from others.

These things are not in alignment with our goals. These situations create storms in our lives whenever we encounter them, and they can appear in all of our lives regardless of who we are, where we came from, or where we're headed in life. They can be present in our lives regardless of where we fall on the socio-economic scale.

We all encounter hundreds of circumstances that can create storms in our lives. They come in all different shapes, sizes, and forms. Some can come and go quickly, and others seem to linger for what seems like an eternity. These storms create challenges in our lives and can make going forward with our goals difficult for us.

I related earlier how during my freshman year in college I arrived on campus with a bang and became a starter as a defensive back at the University of Texas. My goal at that time was to get a college education, have a great college football career, and ultimately go on to play in the National Football League. Everything was going really well, and then I was injured and missed playing in all but four games during that season. That was a difficult challenge for me.

However, life was about to get a lot tougher for me. That's because during that same period in my freshman year, I received a call from my mom informing me that one of my older brothers, the one right next to me in age, had been in an automobile accident. His injuries were so severe that he needed special care and was placed in a hospital in Austin, right near the University of Texas campus. I could literally look out of my dorm room window and see the location of the hospital where he was receiving treatment. He lived for a couple of months before he passed away from his injuries.

Each circumstance in our life brings about a different emotion within us that causes us to react in a certain way. The passing of my brother was unlike anything I had ever experienced in my life. He was the first one of my brothers or sisters to pass away. During that time, all I felt was a lot of pain.

Today, when I look back on this happening, I realize that the passing of my brother was neither a roadblock, an obstacle, a barrier, nor a setback or failure; it was the loss of a loved one. Without a doubt, it was one of the most difficult circumstances I had ever faced in my life. One which it took a great deal of time, prayer, patience, forgiveness, and healing to overcome. And I say forgiveness because after his passing I felt guilty because he was located so close to me while he was in the hospital, and I felt I should have visited him more often. My guilt subsided only with prayer, healing, and forgiveness over a long period of time.

While I was growing up, my mom always said there would be tough times ahead. There's no doubt that this was a really hard time for me. The combination of circumstances surrounding my being away from home for the first time, my brother's passing, the guilt I was feeling, and things not going as planned in football with my injury added up to the fact that I endured one of the most challenging periods of my life. Through it all, I was able to make the adjustment of being away from home for the first time, overcoming my injury, and with patience and healing over time deal with my brother's passing, but it was hard.

I knew back then, and I really know today that closing the gaps in our lives is hard. That's because at some point or another in our lives, we all will have to deal with hurtful or unfavorable circumstances, things not going as planned, or negative comments we hear from other people. No one is immune to these three things in life. These situations create storms in our lives, some of which are severe.

Highly effective people encounter these kinds of circumstances as well. Some life events are more dramatic than others; each circumstance brings out a different emotion within us, causing us to react a certain way. If our reactions, decisions, or actions are not aligned with our aims in life, the storms can hinder our ability to take the necessary steps to close the gap in our lives.

As difficult as it may be because of the situation we find ourselves in, by being proactive in our responses to the circumstances we're facing at the time, we can actually write the script in our lives. We can do so, although it may be one of the hardest things we ever have to do. And if we invite God to be our coauthor, the script of our lives will read much better.

I believe there's a God. I also believe that God does not place limitations on any of us. We either place them on ourselves or we allow others to place them on us.

It's not the storms we encounter in life that ultimately make the difference between success and failure because we all encounter them—it's how we deal with them and how well-focused we remain on our goal.

It's not the circumstances we find ourselves in today or the negative comments we hear from others that can hinder us; it's our reactions to them that can get in the way of us achieving our goals. It's not the fact that things are not going as planned that knocks us off our goal but our reactions and the decisions we make to those things that can get in the way of closing the gap.

Our reactions to the storms in our lives are based on the way we have been conditioned to think, believe, and behave. That's because something is guiding, directing, or controlling us in life. These drivers are based in part on our subconscious beliefs.

When we encounter a storm in life, we may react a certain way based on our perception of what may have caused the storm or the circumstances surrounding it. Based on our subconscious beliefs, the storm may cause us to emotionally react in a manner consistent with the way we think, behave, or react to things in life. This is why it's wise to occasionally ask ourselves, or ask our loved ones the question; "How do we respond to things when our expectations are not met?"

That's because our beliefs, habits, attitudes, and expectations often determine our reactions to the storms in our lives. If we feel we have been victimized by someone and fail to forgive that person or ourselves, then any time we are reminded of that situation we may react in a resentful, angry, or guilty manner. And if we continue to react in this manner, these behavioral patterns will soon feel normal. They will be what we get used to in life. If these behavioral patterns are out of alignment with our mission, vision, purpose, goals, and values in life, they can potentially hinder our ability to close the gap in our lives, especially when things get hard for us.

The question becomes how are we supposed to respond when things get hard in life? We will cover that in the next chapter.

CHAPTER 18

HOW TO RESPOND WHEN THINGS GET HARD

When things get hard or tough for us in life, that's when we have to be at our best in bringing true meaning to character words like courage, focus, faith, forgiveness, commitment, patience, resilience, and others when we need to apply them. That's how we need to respond when things get hard for us. The better we are at taking these steps, the closer we can move ourselves to the attainment of our goals in life.

One of the greatest blessings I realized from playing sports, especially at the professional level, did not take place necessarily on the field. It was the opportunity to study firsthand the billionaire owners in terms of what really enabled them to not just be successful team owners but successful private business owners in their chosen fields or professions. It was studying their business practice for success.

Playing pro sports provided me with an opportunity to take the life lessons learned from studying billionaire owners and playing with and against some of the world's greatest athletes on a daily basis and transfer those insights to the World Class Coaches platform. I focused especially on the things I learned about how these people responded in their respective spaces when things got hard for them.

At World Class Coaches, we believe that each of us in God's kingdom was born with unique gifts and talents. We also believe that each of us is guided by a purposeful mission and vision in life or the pursuit of that which brings us the greatest degree of inner peace, self-fulfillment, and self-satisfaction.

At World Class Coaches, we seek to take steps to equip people, teams, and organizations with the means to unleash more of their natural God-given potential, regardless of their gifts or talents or what field or profession they may be in.

That is what playing sports is all about; however, this is also what my mom was teaching us kids while raising her children as a single parent in La Grange. It's about being the best you can be, regardless of your chosen field or profession despite circumstances, things not going as planned in life, negative comments you hear from others, or how hard things get for you.

One of the most valuable lessons I learned from sports was how to tap into my healthy competitive spirit to bring true meaning to character words like courage, focus, patience, commitment, persistence, resilience, and others when I needed to apply them. Specifically, to assist in closing the gap in my life when things were hard. And I had to do so on a daily basis against the world's greatest competition and in a hostile environment. However, this is also what my mom was teaching us growing up as kids in La Grange.

Another one of my takeaways from playing sports was understanding that regardless of what sector of society you operate in, there is a set of basic fundamentals that apply to that space. For example, in football they are blocking, tackling, and protecting the football.

In football at any level, from youth football to the NFL, the team that skillfully practices the basic fundamentals of the game the best will usually put themselves in the best position for success in achieving their goals. This is especially the case over the course of a season. The teams that usually compete for the championship in their respective sport are the ones that most consistently practice the basic fundamentals of their sport. They do so regardless of how hard things get for them when they come up against great competition in the championship game. The same principle applies to all sectors of society and to all age groups.

Once I served as a volunteer youth sports coach. One of my goals with the team was for them to thoroughly understand the basic fundamentals of the game and confidently and skillfully practice them consistently on a daily basis no matter what the circumstances.

To achieve our goal, I taught them the five basic football fundamentals I used as a pro football player. These included: 1) tackle well, 2) be a sound blocker, 3) protect the football, 4) run full speed at all times, and 5) have fun playing the game. I had one basic rule for the team: "To be the best you can be no matter what the circumstances."

The tenet to "run full speed" was an attempt to remove the hesitation from their play. Some kids have a tendency to hesitate before their every move for various reasons.

For example, some of the kids would say during a practice, "Hey coach, I'm tired."

When they did, I would simply reply by asking them, "What does being tired have to do with running full speed?"

Often, they would say, "Well nothing."

I would reply by saying, "Well running full speed is running full speed, whether you're tired or not. So, make sure you have plenty of water, and get back in there and make sure you're running full speed on every play." And off they go learning how to practice success patterns when things get hard.

The exact same scenario would take place if they would say, "Hey coach, I'm hot, or cold, or it's raining,"

I would reply by saying, "What does being hot, or cold, or the fact that it's raining have to do with running full speed?"

They would reply, "Nothing."

What I was teaching them was the importance of remaining focused on practicing the fundamentals of football to the best of their abilities despite the circumstances. My aim was to teach them how to bring true meaning to the character words when they needed to apply them and how to respond when things got hard for them.

Another reason why you sometimes see hesitation in children participating in activities is usually because the kids fear making a mistake and having their coaches or parents embarrass them by verbally communicating their displeasure in front of all their friends. Managing expectations, both my own as their coach and theirs and those of their parents was one of my primary duties and responsibilities as a youth coach.

When kids are managing these expectations, things can become extremely difficult for them. It's often difficult for your son or daughter to live up to your expectations as their parents.

That's because kids naturally learn to seek approval from their coaches or parents for their performance. It's also a problem because parents unwittingly develop in their kids the need to please and the need for approval from others but show or express their frustrations by the way they communicate to them when their performance falls short of their expectations.

If the parent continues to verbally react in a critical manner, the child may feel that he or she is unable to live up to the parents' expectations. As a result, they become conditioned to think a certain way about themselves, and they react accordingly. After a while, they may develop negative beliefs and carry these with them.

Often these beliefs, which may not be properly aligned with their aims in life, can make closing the gap difficult once they become adults unless they decide they can and want to change them. This problem is especially evident when things get hard for them.

Some of the beliefs we hold today come from our parents or other authority figures who have expressed their displeasure at our performance during dance practices or soccer games or other activities. Children may be told by parents, other authority figures, teachers, or relatives that they are "dumb," "can't get anything right," "can't draw," "aren't good at sports," or are "clumsy" over and over again. As they continue to hear these negative statements, they begin to lock on to those limited or false beliefs — and then act on the basis of them, especially when they run into twists, turns, and roadblocks in life.

Another way we can "lock on" to a mistaken belief about ourselves may be how we perceive our performance in a particular situation. If we look back on our lives, we might recall a situation where, whether we were prepared or not, we did not perform as well as expected, and someone called us out on it. And we may have believed after that incident that we lacked the ability to perform as expected.

As a result, we now try to avoid repeating that same experience, and that avoidance tendency affects the way we think! We impose limitations on ourselves—limitations that do not reflect our true God-given gifts and talents but more accurately reflect how we've learned to think about ourselves and those around us. We then become used to certain things in life — things that can make closing the gap in our lives difficult if they're not properly aligned with our mission, vision, purpose, goals, and values in life.

When things get difficult for you to proceed in the right direction in life, I encourage you to constantly assess why you may be thinking the way you're thinking. If you're not realizing the results you are seeking, ask yourself, "What is holding me back from achieving my goals?" Or ask yourself, "What's holding me back from closing the gap in my life?" These are steps highly effective people take to assist putting themselves in the best position to achieve their goals.

Another reason why it's important to take these steps is because by going in the other direction we can place limitations on ourselves in so many different ways. In addition to limiting ourselves based on our fear of not performing as expected, we should be constantly asking ourselves how else we might be limiting ourselves in the way we think? What might be some other limited beliefs that prevent us from realizing more of our God-given potential and achieving more of our goals? How might we be reaffirming those limited beliefs, which may be making things difficult to close the gap in our lives?

For example, how often do you say, "I'm a really shy person," or "I'm just not good at that," or "I can't afford that." or "I can't do that." These are examples of negative affirmations that some people use daily without understanding the impact they have on their belief system and their performance.

I encourage you to become more aware of the strength of these type of affirmations — statements of beliefs that you continually tell yourself. Our subconscious mind accepts what we affirm and works to carry it out for us. Our mind accepts a belief until we change it. Even a one-time affirmation by another person can have a huge impact on our behavior.

For example, the world is full of rites of passage. When you graduate from college, you're awarded a diploma, which certifies that you've met the school's educational requirements. After certification, you are expected to play the designated role in whatever space you operate in. A would-be doctor goes to medical school and after fulfilling all the requirements to become a doctor, he or she is granted a license to practice medicine. Yesterday, you were just a medical student, but today after a rite of passage, you're a doctor. If you had a medical condition that required treatment, how comfortable would you feel having a medical student treat you as opposed to someone with a medical license who had been practicing for some time? Not very comfortable I would think.

I encourage you to assess what enables someone not to be educated one day and then receive a diploma and be educated the next day — to be a medical student one day and a doctor the next day. Without making light of the process it takes to become a doctor, think about what really transpires to cause the change in our belief system and expectations by which we live our lives. In this case, there is a certification process that validates the rite of passage. This is vital because of the role authority figures play in our lives.

Last but certainly not least, one of the things I learned from playing sports was exactly the same thing I've learned over my entire lifetime. I learned it from my mom and all the professors, teachers, coaches, mentors, and other authority figures in my life, both in sports and in everyday life.

I've learned that there's a reason why kids have parents, students have professors and teachers, and professional athletes across all sports, male and female, have coaches. They are the purpose-driven authority figures in our lives. These experts help keep us focused on the fundamental activities necessary to close the gap in our lives, despite negative circumstances, things not going as planned, or critical comments we hear from others. They are there to assist us through tough times when things get hard in life.

When I first set a goal to play in the National Football League when I was 13 years old, I did not know that no one from La Grange had ever played in the League before. Well, I shared my goal with my uncle. Now without a doubt, I know he had my best interests in mind when he said to me, "Johnnie, it's in your own best interest that I do not want you to set your goal that high because I don't want you to be disappointed when you don't make it."

As a 13-year old when I heard those comments I thought how nice, my uncle really loves me, and he truly did. He loved me so much that he did not want me to be disappointed.

I kept what he said to myself, until things got difficult for me, and I started to doubt myself. I did not necessarily doubt my goal, because it was so far away. However, it was during one of my conversations with my mom that I decided to share what my uncle said to me. I said, "Mom, my uncle said I couldn't play in the NFL."

And my mom, who knew very little about football or the League, politely and confidentially said, "Well is your uncle God?"

And I said, "No."

She replied, "Well then why are you listening to him?" And with that, she refocused me back on my goal. When things get hard or you start to doubt yourself, that's the time to refocus on your goals and practice the basic fundamental activities necessary to assist you in achieving them.

Since that day, I have had many similar experiences when key authority figures in my life have refocused me at a time when I needed it the most. Those steps have enabled me to remain focused on practicing the necessary fundamental activities to close the gap in my life, especially when I encounter storms along the way.

Start Where You Are	Success Habit Patterns	Driven by a Higher Purpose	Clarify Your Current Reality	When Vision Becomes Reality		

SECTION

5

WHEN VISION BECOMES REALITY

When your vision becomes a reality, your mission, purpose, goals, and values are brought to life. When this takes place, you close the gap in your life. Along the way you change the way you view the world in areas where you desire to grow personally and professionally. You take steps to align your beliefs, habits, attitudes, and expectations with your vision. You unlock your mind and unleash more of your God-given potential. You "lock on" to what you want to accomplish (your circle of focus) and "lock out" things that are out of your control. During the process, every day you move one step closer to achieving your goals, whether you realize it or not.

CHAPTER 19

LIFE EXPERIENCES SHAPE OUR WORLD AND INSPIRE OUR LIFE'S MISSION

One of the most fulfilling meetings I've had in my adult life took place right after I purchased my mom the brick home she had envisioned owning when I was kid. I completely furnished the home, and after I presented her the keys, I told her that she had worked hard enough in life in assisting her children to be the best they could be. I informed her that, from that point forward, it was now our turn as her children to be there for her.

One of my goals was for her to not have any worries. It was my desire for her to live the rest of her life filled with freedom of choice in terms of where and how she spent her time, with a purpose. A life filled with peace!

To assist in accomplishing my goal, I met with her to discuss her expenses. I asked her what household expenses she had related to the house that I was not aware of. Since she had no debt, she basically only had household and living expenses.

That was with the exception of a bunch of insurance policies. She had a small juvenile insurance policy on each of her children. When I asked what they were for, she replied, "In the event I lose one of you, I want to be able to put you to rest with all the love, dignity, and respect you deserve." When she said that to me, I almost lost it; I was overwhelmed.

Then she shared a life insurance policy she had on herself. When I asked her about that one, she replied by saying, "If I happened to pass before you kids, I want you to be able to put me to rest with the same love and dignity; and, whatever is left over, share that among all the children." When she shared that with me, I did lose it.

I lost it for several reasons – her love, her caring for the family, and her thoughtfulness. But the main reason I lost it was because of my remembrance of my older brother's funeral my freshman year in college. I knew that during that time period, we were very poor as a family. Yet, my brother had one of the most beautiful and elaborate funerals I had ever seen in the area. At the time, I did not know how she afforded it. I knew then how she afforded it.

Needless to say, this experience, beginning with my brother's death, his funeral, and culminating with my mom's sharing her reasoning behind the insurance policies, has played a role in shaping how I see the world today. Specifically, providing long-term protection for my family despite the circumstances. Today, I encourage all families to take similar steps in their lives.

My mom made a difference in the lives of her children and the people she came in contact with in her own special way. That was part of her mission and purpose in life.

It's a part of my mission and purpose in life to make a difference in the lives of the people World Class Coaches has the plea-
sure and honor of serving, specifically, when they're going through
phases of transition and change in their lives. My life experiences
have not only helped shaped the way I see the world, they continue to inspire my mission and purpose in life.

I recall having a conversation with one of my good friends
and former teammates with the Rams, Leroy Irvin. I remember it
vividly for several reasons. It took place around 8:00 p.m., during
the evening, when he said, "Hey Johnnie, I just signed with the
Detroit Lions."

This is not unusual, because as players we understand that
changing teams is just part of the game, so I replied by saying,
"Wow, that's great, when do you have to be there?"

He replied, "Tomorrow."

I said, "You're kidding me, what about your family?"

And he replied, "I don't know about them yet, we will have to
figure that out, but I have to be there tomorrow."

You see, he had a wife and three young kids. Knowing them
the way I knew them, I remember thinking to myself, "You know
what, that's got to be really hard on his family."

As professional athletes, this kind of change is normal for our
world. We're accustomed to players and coaches changing teams;
players via trades, free agent signings, and other means. However,
I will never forget that conversation because I had seen that kind of
change take place so many times before in my life. However, it was
different with Leroy's specific experience. It was different because
of my previous life experiences with families moving or relocating
outside of football.

When I shared my life's mission and vision with my life coach,
he asked me how large I wanted my playing field to be? I told
him the world. At that time, he suggested I gain some business
experience in some other profession other than football. I chose
residential real estate sales as the vehicle to gain that experience.

For the last three years of my NFL career, I played pro football, continued studying billionaires and world class athletes, worked on developing the World Class Coaches coaching platform, and sold real estate, all in pursuit of my mission, vision, and purpose in life.

It was my work as a real estate salesperson, combined with watching the life experiences of players and coaches changing teams, that led me to the realization of the impact the natural phases of transition and change has on families, especially those with young children. That is the case across all sectors of society, regardless of your chosen field or where you may fall on the socio-economic scale.

Unfortunately, moving or relocating is a normal part of the various phases of transition and change we all go through in life. Annually, there are approximately 10 million children, ages 19 and younger, who move or relocate with their parents throughout the United States, according to the U.S. Census. There are millions more who go through the same experience worldwide.

Knowing this to be the case and relying on many of my life experiences and my mission, vision, and purpose in life that were at the forefront of my mind, I created the Moving Families Initiative, an awareness, education, and connectivity movement for which World Class Coaches serves as the facilitator. Our aim with the Initiative is to assist parents moving or relocating by making the move less stressful for their entire family via a one-stop access process. A specific focus is placed on assisting their children, ages 19 and younger, in dealing with the physical and emotional challenges of changing neighborhoods, schools, and friends, whether they're moving across town or across the country.

Our commitment to serve, protect, and meet the needs of the Initiative's parents' entire family during periods of transition and change in their lives, with a specific focus on protection for their children, extends to the child's grandparents, aunts, uncles and cousins when necessary.

Our overall aim is to provide families access to high quality education, children's extracurricular activities, affordable housing, and economic opportunities when they move or relocate.

When we look at the world today, there's one thing we see, and that's massive change on many fronts. Change from the way we communicate with each other (social media, and more) – to the way we shop (online), – to the way we use the Internet and other technology to meet many of our needs or gain access to our desired forms of entertainment.

You know things are changing when we are talking about self-driving cars and trucks for the rest of our lives, and our children's lives, and their children's lives.

When we look at the world today, we see change; however, there's one aspect that will always remain the same. That's the fact that life is a continual process of transition and change. When the time arrives we naturally move to the next phase of our lives, whether we're ready for it or not. Along the way, our life experiences will shape the way we see the world, and for many of us they will inspire our mission, vision, and purpose in life.

Another aspect of life today is that we may be closer than we think to achieving our goals whether we realize it or not. One of the reasons why is access and connectivity – as in the resources that are available to us. Resources that may assist us in removing many of the obstacles or barriers standing in the way of us achieving our goals disappear with the click of a mouse or one phone call. That's the case if we know how to access those resources and have the right skill set to assist us in achieving our goals, a skill set enhanced by a good quality education.

One of the overall aims of the MFI is to provide families access to high-quality education when they move or relocate. Whether you're a parent looking for a quality school system for your children during their pre-K to 12th grade school years, or you have a high school graduate looking to go to college, or whether your child decides to go back to college later in life, the organization has resources available. More so today than ever before, a high-quality education will enable you to better utilize many tools and resources that are available to you to assist you in closing the gap in your life.

I understand it will not be easy. In fact, there's a high probability that it will be hard because of all of the change taking place in the world and all of the choices and options we have available to assist us in meeting our needs or achieving our goals.

Because life can be challenging at times, parents often set a goal to instill certain life skills, character traits, and values in their children when they're growing up. I was not aware of it at that time; however, when I look back, that's exactly what my mom was doing when she was communicating her one-liners to her children when we were kids.

That's also what Mrs. Mayer, my algebra teacher in high school, was doing when she pulled me into her classroom, and said, "Johnnie, I understand you're a really good football player." "I want you to know that I expect you to give me the same level of commitment and effort in my class that you give your coaches on the football field."

I consider my mom and Mrs. Mayer to be among the best parents and school teachers this world has ever had to offer. They're excellent in teaching critical life skills, character traits and values. The teachings provided by the likes of my mom and the Mrs. Mayer's of the world are valuable at every stage of the process.

As previously mentioned, participating in extracurricular activities provides kids with a built-in platform that greatly enhances their ability to learn these valuable teachings firsthand. Their participation provides them with a purposeful platform to build character and enhance life skills and values that they may be difficult to find and learn elsewhere. Their participation can also assist them in developing new friendships in a safe environment when they move or relocate to a new community, neighborhood, or school.

Learning these tenets the correct way at an early age is irreplaceable. It's equally valuable to make sure that we continue working to grow in these areas as we journey through life, but especially when we're going through phases of transition and change. That's because we will need to learn how to apply these principles time and time again when we run into obstacles or barriers that can hinder our ability to close the gap in our lives and achieve the goals we've set for ourselves.

That's certainly the case with college graduates seeking to transition from being a college student to everyday life. These young adults are well-educated with college degrees.

World Class Coaches conducts random assessments of the audiences we serve. In one of the studies, we assessed male and female college graduates in their journey from college life to everyday life. We assessed young adults ranging from new graduates to those who have been out of school for at least 10 years.

We asked the graduates five basic questions revolving around the various phases of transitions they may be experiencing at present or have experienced in their lives, beginning with their transition from college to everyday life. Graduates were asked to include subsequent transitions they may be have gone through or may be presently experiencing.

The participants were asked the following five questions. Following each question are the most common responses recorded.

1. What are your primary personal and professional goal(s) you're looking to accomplish as you go through this phase of transition in your life?

    • Find the right economic vehicle to achieve my goals,

    • Find affordable housing,

    • Paying off student loans.

2. What are your greatest needs, which if met, will enable you to achieve your primary goal(s) in life?

    • Clarity on what type of business opportunities are available,

    • Improving leadership skills,

- Clarity of skills required to create and manage a profitable business,
- Access to business leaders for guidance in creating a successful business.

3. What obstacles or barriers do you perceive to be standing in the way of you achieving your primary goal(s)?
   - Limited business network or mentors,
   - Limited business knowledge and limited understanding of what it takes to create a business,
   - Time/Timing,
   - Lack of capital/equity for sustainability,
   - No visibility = lack of customers or clients.

4. What skills do you believe you need to improve in yourself to assist you in achieving your goal(s)?
   - Patience and confidence to realize the new skills learned will take time.

5. What do you believe are your greatest challenges facing you today as you go through this specific transition in your life?
   - Adjusting to a new environment,
   - Learning how to be successful at new job,
   - Learning a new business.

As I look at the responses of the participants, I can relate to them. When I read them, I often think of my life experiences revolving around the people I observed going through various phases of transition and change in their lives, specifically during my college, pro football, and real estate sales careers. Their responses inspire part of my mission, vision, and purpose with the MFI.

Two of our aims with the Initiative are to provide families access to affordable housing and economic opportunities via a one-stop process when they move or relocate while they are going through a phase of transition and change in their lives.

The MFI's definition and purpose of affordable housing takes on a slightly different meaning and purpose than the one commonly deemed affordable by the government. The latter definition is commonly thought of as access to low-income housing.

To the MFI, affordable housing is used to describe parents moving or relocating with young children and gaining access to housing by renting or owning their own homes, regardless of whether your income level is at the low, middle, or upper income bracket. It's about gaining access to a desired area, city, or neighborhood where they can take steps to achieve their ultimate goal or goals of gaining access to a specific school system for their children or whatever other reason that is driving their need or desire to move or relocate. Our aim with the Initiative is to assist people in taking that step, with a specific focus on assisting their children in dealing with the challenges of moving.

In addition, we know from the results of the college graduate assessments that two of the greatest needs recent college graduates face are finding affordable housing and economic opportunities in the city, area, or state in which they choose to pursue their goals. Our aim is to assist them in overcoming the obstacles and barriers standing in the way of them taking steps to achieve their goals in these areas as they transition to the next phase of their lives after college.

Economic opportunities are all about finding the right economic vehicle, strong business relationships, and connectivity to assist you in meeting your financial needs and achieving your financial goals. They are also about taking steps to close the gap between where you are today and your ultimate aims in life.

There's that old saying, "It's not about what you know, it's about who you know." Economic opportunities are all about who you know. They are about connecting with the right relationships to assist you in finding and building a successful economic vehicle that will support you in accomplishing your overall aims in life.

It is one of the MFI's overall aims to provide students grad-uating from college access to affordable housing and economic opportunities, one step at a time. With each step, they move closer to achieving their goals of meeting their financial needs and achieving their future financial goals despite certain circumstances.

Life has not always been easy for me. But that's the case for each of us. My life experiences have shaped the way I see the world, and they continue to inspire my mission and purpose in life.

CHAPTER 20

CHANGE THE WAY YOU VIEW THE WORLD

The world is changing at a rapid pace, and it's changing right before our eyes. As it continues to change, there's a need for us to change the way we view it, especially when we're going through a natural phase of transition and change in our lives. That includes changing the way we see ourselves. I understand that this can be difficult for many of us.

One of the greatest coaching suggestions I've received in my life was when my life coach suggested that I gain some business experience in some area of my life other than sports (football). Up until I took that step, I saw myself as a professional athlete. My entire life was centered around being a pro football player. That is how I saw the world, and that is how I felt the world saw me.

Taking this step first caused me to evaluate the way I viewed the world. And although it was not easy, it caused me to begin the process of viewing the world differently than I was accustomed to seeing it.

As I began taking steps to officially transition from football to everyday life and a business orientation, I knew that if I were to realize my mission, vision, purpose, and goals in life, I would need to gain the business experience my life coach suggested. This required me to change the way I viewed the world and to explore viable options aligned with my life's aims,

How do you view the world today as it relates to your mission, vision, purpose, goals, and values? How do you view yourself? How do you view others around you? Your life experiences will contribute to how you see the world.

Because we see the world the way that we see it, there are occasions when we may be closer than we think to achieving our goals in life, and we may just not realize it. In many instances, just a slight shift in the way we think may enable us to become more of a thinker who considers more options, to think outside our current limitations. For this reason, I encourage you to be as creative and innovative as you can be to realize your aims; however, I encourage you to do so within the confines of your mission, vision, purpose, and values in life.

This process will enable us to see the answers to the problems or our way around the obstacles on our way to achieving our goals. It will enable us to see with more focus and clarity those options and opportunities when they appear while pursuing our goals.

This brings us to a key point about being closer to achieving our goals than we think. When we set a goal, the opportunities to accomplish it may be present, but we may not have seen them yet. The bigger the goal, the more difficult it may be for us to see the opportunities.

The question is what might prevent us from seeing things as clearly as we desire when opportunities present themselves to us? One barrier is our natural filtering system—our senses.

We naturally filter things through our five senses of taste, sound, sight, touch, and smell. Based on how we've been conditioned to see the world and our life experiences, we see the world through a certain lens. Because of this we've developed blind spots that may prevent us from seeing the various options we may need to see to remain focused on our goals, although these options may be right in front of us.

How well we deal with blind spots will determine how well we remain focused on our goals. We may not even know that we have them. One way we can recognize that someone may have a blind spot is when we hear them saying, "This doesn't make any sense to me," or "I don't get it."

Unless we're ready, willing, and able to change the way we view the world, blind spots can be a serious shortcoming! Marriages fail because people have blind spots. Friendships often dissolve because of blind spots. Businesses often fail because their leaders have blind spots. We all have blind spots.

Although we all have blind spots, highly effective people seem to have fewer than people who perform at a lower level. That's because they learn to change the way they view the world, as needed, to remain focused on their goals.

For many highly effective people, it's a part of their approach to be on a constant search for a better way to accomplish their goals. They recognize that they may not see all that they need to see, and they are analytical in their approach to life. They question those things that conflict with their beliefs or points of view in a positive and constructive manner as they search for the answers to their questions or for means to realize their goals.

Seeing all that we need to see and eliminating our blind spots have little to do with how smart we are or how gifted or talented we are. But it has a lot to do with how we think, what we believe, and how we view the world.

There are times when if we're able to change the way we see the world, we may actually benefit from having blind spots. Setting a goal allows us to "lock-on" to that goal and "lock-out" needless distractions. So, as we "lock-on" to a goal with clarity, we can focus wisely on achieving the goal while locking-out needless distractions` that may hinder us from achieving our goal.

This is a tremendous advantage to have. You need to be careful, however, as one of our greatest strengths could become one of our most potent weaknesses. Our ability to "lock-on" to a goal could cause us to overlook potential valuable options that may be available to assist us in realizing our goals. This is because of our life experiences and the way we view the world.

Many of us may leave out important parts of reality because we are conditioned to think a certain way and see things a certain way. If we become overly locked on to an idea or approach we can entirely "lock-out" another possibly more creative or productive option.

Once we "lock-on" to an opinion, belief, or attitude about ourselves or someone else, it becomes difficult to see or understand things that may conflict with these beliefs or opinions. We become less aware or perhaps completely unaware of an alternative way of seeing things.

This "blindness" can make seeing the world in a different way difficult because we tend to think about one thing at a time and to receive only information that will validate our point of view. The key is to know when to "lock-on" and when to "lock-out."

So I encourage you to change the way you view the world when you encounter storms in your life and to become an option thinker — someone who is searching for a better, more effective way of realizing your goals and living the life you desire. This ability will enable you to remain focused on your goals, even in the midst of the storm. By taking this step, you will move closer to achieving your goals in life.

CHAPTER 21

THE TRUTH AS WE SEE IT

Have you ever wondered how two people can look at the same thing and see two different things? Well, not only do we tend to think about one thing at a time but often when we look at certain things in life we tend to receive only information that will validate our point of view. One of the contributing factors to why we operate this way is because we tend to see the truth as we see it through our lens. This may not be the whole truth, or even the real truth, but it's the truth as we see it. And this can affect how we perform in certain aspects of life.

During my NFL career, each year we would begin the season by reporting to training camp. We took this step to prepare for the upcoming season. It's a step every single sports team takes each year.

Every year when we arrived at camp, we knew that once the regular season started, there would be a possibility that we might lose 25% to 40% of our games and still have a chance to win the Super Bowl. The same applied for every team in the NFL.

When you look at all professional sports, the same ratios are true. In Major League Baseball, teams that qualify for the playoffs each year may lose 40% or more of their games and still have a chance to win the World Series. The same applies for the National Basketball Association. In the NBA, the teams that qualify for the playoffs year after year may lose 40% or more of their games and still have a chance to win the NBA Championship.

On the flip side, when you look at the teams that perform the worst each year across all sports, they may lose 60% or more of their games. The question in professional sports, where the system is designed to create parity throughout all the leagues, is why do you have teams performing on two ends of the spectrum? They all have super high-quality professional players.

Part of the reason can be found in the way they view and practice the basic fundamentals of their sport, especially when they encounter the natural twists, turns, and roadblocks that lead to storms along the way. Their approach to understanding and consistently performing the basic fundamentals of their profession is the truth as they see it.

Of all the professions in society, professional sports may provide us with the best platform and certainly the most visible one on which to watch players and teams' true beliefs translate into reality. The team and its players that most consistently practice the fundamentals of their profession better than their opponents usually qualify for the playoffs.

When the playoffs begin in each sport, a new season commences involving the best performers over the course of the past season competing for the championship. Because this is the best of the best competing against each other, it becomes crystal clear to all participants that they must consistently practice the basic fundamentals better than their opponents. This enables them to put themselves in the best position for success in achieving their goals.

But that's only part of it. Another key element is their belief that they are indeed champions and deserving of winning the title. That is the truth as they see it. Once the playoffs begin, there's usually a favorite to win the championship in their sport. That team not always, but often wins the championship. They do so because they not only see themselves as champions (the truth as they see it), but they also consistently practice the championship fundamentals and habit patterns of their profession better than their opponents throughout the playoffs.

Highly effective people come from all walks of life and from all levels of the socio-economic scale. They consistently practice the championship basic fundamental habit patterns of their profession better than their competition in their chosen field regardless of what space they operate in. This is due in part to their beliefs and the development of critical thinking skills by many of these highly effective individuals and the proper alignment of their behavioral patterns with their aims in life.

The same applies to highly effective people in sales. The individuals or teams that consistently practice championship basic fundamentals of their profession better than their competition will put themselves in the best position to achieve their goals.

In sales, as in sports, we're going to have some days where things are just not going to go well. We're going to run into all sort of twists, turns, and roadblocks along the way. The question is how are we going to handle them and remain focused on our goals? The key is found in our beliefs, the development of our critical thinking skills, and the proper alignment of our behavioral patterns with our aims in life regardless of our profession.

When this is applied to our economic vehicle, it provides us a unique opportunity to move one step closer to achieving our goals. That's because as consumers in life, we all have needs we desire to meet or goals to achieve. These needs or goals are met or achieved by the products, services, or entertainment we provide to the marketplace through our economic vehicle. We deliver them through the development of business relationships with the people we serve.

As we covered earlier, business relationships are built on three things: consumer needs, goals, and timing. Timing is important on many fronts in life; however, it's vital in the creation and the ongoing growth and development of business relationships. When the timing is right for all of us as consumers, we take steps to meet our needs or achieve our goals.

Business relationships are driven by the needs and goals of the consumer. They're powered by our passion and purpose in life to assist consumers in meeting their needs and in achieving their goals with our economic vehicle.

Because we live in a world where it's common for product, service, and entertainment providers to compete for the same consumers in their space, it's extremely important to align our passion and purpose in life with our economic vehicle. Often it shows in our interaction with consumers; however, where it really shows is in our commitment to taking the necessary steps to assist consumers in meeting their specific needs and achieving their goals while maintaining the values of our economic vehicle.

We will know when we find the alignment we're looking for because we will experience a greater degree of inner peace, self-fulfillment, and self-satisfaction in life. In addition, special blessings will begin coming our way to assist us in meeting our own personal needs and achieving our objectives consistent with our personal and professional mission, vision, purpose, and goals in life.

Today, I encourage you to assess for proper alignment between your beliefs and your mission, vision, purpose, goals, and values. You're looking for the truth as you see it today. Taking this step will enable you to make sure your beliefs are properly aligned with your aims in life, and you can see yourself as a champion. With it, you move one step closer to achieving your goals in life.

As a professional athlete, I believed that I was one of the top players in the League at my position. Regardless of what type of storm I encountered, I would not change my beliefs about myself as a professional athlete. As a peak performance coach, I believe equally as strongly in my coaching abilities. Of course, I have been coached all my life.

That was not the case when I first became a real estate professional. In fact, it may have been the opposite. I did not have the same beliefs or confidence about myself as a real estate professional.

Although, I did not possess the same beliefs in real estate that I had in football or peak performance coaching, I still set high goals for myself as a real estate professional. Since I understood the importance of goal setting from my athletic training, I set a goal to be closing a minimum of 100 transactions a year in real estate by the time I retired from the NFL. When I look back on things, I am not certain where the number 100 came from. I do recall that it sounded good. I felt that if I accomplished my annual real estate goals, I would make a difference in life by helping that number of people meet their needs and achieve their goals.

After we set a goal, we naturally desire to achieve it; we want to hit the target we're aiming for. However, if we don't really believe we can accomplish it, there's a good chance that one of the twists, turns, or roadblocks we may encounter along the way could hinder us in attaining our goals. I was very aware of this and knew that one of the most important steps I needed to take in seeking to accomplish my real estate goals was to assess my beliefs for proper alignment with my mission, vision, purpose, goals, and values. I knew that if I was going to utilize my potential in real estate and if I had any chance of attaining my goals, I needed to change my beliefs to be more in alignment with someone who closes 100 transactions per year. That's because our beliefs about ourselves can be our most powerful allies or our most potent enemies.

When you look around today, there are people who appear to have enormous potential. Unfortunately, although blessed with these exceptional gifts and talents, many of them appear to be using only a small portion of their God-given potential. Why is this?

I believe that in part it's because of the way they have learned to think about themselves and the world around them. Many have become limited thinkers. We limit ourselves based on our beliefs.

The way we think and the way others have learned to think about us can hinder us in the accomplishment of our goals if we do not know how to effectively deal with it. This is why I encourage you to consistently evaluate why you think the way you do and ensure your beliefs are in alignment with your aims in life. While we have great God-given potential, we may not behave in a way that reflects those wonderful gifts. In fact, we may not even realize how much potential we're blessed with.

That's because we act in accordance with "the truth" as we believe it or perceive it to be, not the real truth. We act in accordance with what we think "the truth" is — even if, in reality, we are mistaken.

For example, while growing up we may have been conditioned to believe certain things about ourselves: "We're good in sports, but not good in math." "We're good in academics, but not good in sports." Our parents or authority figures made it clear what they thought about us. We were told over and over again, in words and by the way we were treated, that we were smart or dumb, athletic or clumsy, dependable or lazy, trustworthy or unreliable, valuable and worthy of respect or worthless and deserving of punishment.

We may have grown up without a mother or father in a single-parent household or in an environment where our parents may have been abusive or addicted to alcohol or drugs. Or, we may have grown up in a tough neighborhood where drugs, alcohol, and violence were a way of life. We may have been treated as if we were inferior.

Through it all, our life experiences have shaped the way we view the world. As a child, we had no choice. If we are consistently treated a certain way, after a while we begin to believe it as "the truth." We begin to think and see things that way. That's where the real damage is done. That's where our God-given potential starts to get blocked. After we begin to see it as "the truth," we begin to act like it.

The good news is we can start choosing who we will be and how we will live our lives. I encourage you to search for the truth — the real truth about your God-given potential that allows you to be the best you can be and not those "truths" that are based on what you have been conditioned to believe about yourself: your past failures or experiences, or comments you hear from others who may be operating on limited information or limited thinking.

If you change the way you view the world – the way you think, you may well use more of your potential. If you eliminate your mistaken beliefs about yourself and properly align true beliefs about yourself with your aims in life, you will be better able to remain focused on your goals, even in the midst of a storm. During the process, you move one step closer to achieving your goals in life.

CHAPTER 22

ALIGN BELIEFS, HABITS AND ATTITUDES WITH YOUR AIMS

When I first started in real estate, I had a problem and didn't even know it. That was until my sales trainer suggested I make sales calls. That's when I discovered I had a fear of the telephone.

The group we selected to call were absentee homeowners, which meant they owned a second home they were not presently living in. The group was from our company's past client list, so they were somewhat familiar with my company. We prepared a general call framework to follow, and I blocked off an hour to call the home-owners. The goal was to inquire if they had an interest in selling their home.

Up until that point in my life, there were times when I may have hesitated to call someone but never anything like I was about to experience when seeking to make the sales calls. The first time I picked up the phone to make a call, it felt like it weighed 500 pounds. It felt so heavy I literally had difficulty getting it off the hook. And when I finally did manage to make a call, I often prayed no one would answer on the other end.

Frequently people didn't answer, and that was perfectly okay with me. It may not have been okay with me after I put myself in position to achieve my goal of producing 100 transactions a year, but it was just fine with me and my discomfort while I was making those calls.

That discomfort lasted until one day I made a call and someone answered. When they did, I introduced myself by saying, "Hello, this is Johnnie Johnson," I told them my company's name, and I said, "How are you today?" The gentleman replied, "Fine, how are you?" My heart started racing a million miles per hour from fear and anxiety. I replied by saying, "I'm fine, thank you for asking." I then said, "The purpose of my call is to inquire if you had considered selling your home at such and such property address."

I will never forget what took place next. The gentleman on the other end of phone said, "No, I'm not interested in selling that property; however, I am interested in purchasing another home before the end of the year." That's when I replied, "Ok, well thank you." And I hung the phone up on him.

That's when my trainer asked me, "What happened?" I told him the person I just called said, "He was interested in purchasing another home before the end of the year." To this day, I still remember the look on my trainer's face, when he asked me, "Well, why didn't you help him?" I said, "Because I just hung up on him." When I look back on it, if my trainer had that shocked look on his face when I told him what happened, I can only imagine the look that gentleman I was talking to had on his face when I hung up on him.

This incident made me realize I had a problem. Actually, I had two problems. The first one was my fear. I had to ask myself, what was it I was afraid of? This was all new to me. I would leave my real estate office and go to football practice, where I was very confident. In fact, I may have been the most confident person and player I had been at any point in my life as a football player. But that confidence was not being transferred to my real estate practice.

The other problem was even more alarming when I related it to my football profession. In football, the basic fundamentals of the game are blocking and tackling better than your opponent and protecting the football. I understood them very well. My beliefs, habit patterns, and attitudes were properly aligned with my aims in that profession. However, that was not the case in real estate.

Real estate has its own basic fundamentals. They include making personal contact with prospective customers, earning some of their trust, and based on their needs, goals, and timing, transitioning them into a client.

That brings me to my other problem. I had set a goal to be producing 100 transactions a year by the time I retired from the NFL. The problem was my goal; if I had a habit of hanging up on prospects when they needed my real estate services, that behavior was going to severely conflict with my goal. My beliefs, habit patterns, and attitudes were not properly aligned with my aims. That would not only hinder my ability to hit my goals, it also would hinder my ability to use my full potential in real estate.

I believe that a career in sales is one of the most dynamic and rewarding professions in society today. Salespeople with strong values and a high sense of purpose in serving and meeting the needs of their customers are some of the highest paid and most well-regarded people in any business. One of the greatest challenges in sales is avoiding or recovering from call reluctance. I suffered with this early in my real estate career; I was extremely fearful of communicating with a prospective client on the telephone.

For some of us, our fears are so great at times when seeking to make a sales call that the handset of a telephone may feel like it weighs 500 pounds. For others, they dread making sales calls to such a high degree that they will sometimes go to any extreme to avoid making them, even if they are fully aware that this behavior hinders them in their ability to achieve their goals.

Often people whose lives are driven by fear try desperately to change their behavior. Many have temporary success but soon revert back to where they seem to be most comfortable. This was certainly the case with me at the beginning of my real estate career.

Knowing I had these problems, I began searching for where and how I could change the way I was thinking and behaving in this area. This caused me to think of one of my mom's favorite one liners: "It's not a problem, as long as you can do something about it. The question is what are you going to do about it?" There was no doubt I had a problem, so I decided to take steps to do something about it.

The first step I took was to ask myself a simple question. "What changes do I need to make in my life to put myself in the best position to achieve my goals in real estate, despite circumstances? The immediate answer was, "I needed to properly align my beliefs, habits, and attitudes in real estate with my aims in life. I needed to learn how to practice the basic fundamentals of real estate as consistently and confidently as I practice the fundamentals in football. To take this step, I knew I needed to make changes in my beliefs, habits, patterns, and attitudes toward real estate.

If you feel you're in a similar situation in life, I encourage you to follow my lead, and you, too, will take steps to put yourself in the best position to achieve your goals.

In an effort to better understand how we can effectively deal with making meaningful and lasting change in this area and others, we will take a closer look at why we think and act the way we do. We will examine the thought processes and how our mind works.

My life coach excelled in this area of teaching. Our mind works on two levels: the conscious and the subconscious.

The conscious mind has four basic functions: perceive, associate, evaluate, and decide. The thought process works like this:

First, we see or experience something and **perceive** what we think it may be.

Next, we **associate** what we see with our past, with what we have seen like this before, in an effort to understand it.

Then we analyze and **evaluate** it, asking ourselves: "Is this good or bad for me?" and "What is it leading me toward or away from?" Finally, we **decide** on a course of action based on the information available to us and the beliefs we hold.

Remember that our assessment, analysis, and decision may be based not on an objective truth but rather on our subjective beliefs about what is true.

When I entered the real estate profession, I came in with lots of questions about what it actually took to succeed and about my abilities to perform in the business. Many of the decisions I made early on as a real estate professional were based on comments and information from other people in the real estate industry.

Much of the information I used at that phase of my growth and development was based on these subjective beliefs, and it showed in my approach to the business. I approached the business with fear and self-doubt, which was not the way I approached my life in sports. Although I quickly became aware of this, I experienced some difficulty changing my beliefs in this area. One of the reasons was because of the role of the subconscious mind.

The subconscious mind is composed of two parts: the subconscious and the creative subconscious.

The subconscious acts as a recording mechanism. Like a computer memory bank, it records and stores perceptual data and information. Our subconscious has recorded all our past experiences in life. In addition, it has stored what we think, say, and imagine about ourselves as well as our emotional reactions to those experiences. This adds up to a file of reality we refer to as "the truth as we see it."

However, this "truth" may only be seen through the eyes of the beholder; it is not everyone's truth. It may only be the truth as we perceive it or believe it to be. Thus, our picture of reality may be inaccurate or biased if we compare it to an objective interpretation of reality. We may not have recorded the real truth about our abilities and potential; rather, we have assumed that the habit patterns, attitudes, and opinions about ourselves or others we come in contact with are adequate.

This became very evident to me early on in my real estate career. We all are different in the world. Each of us is unique in our own way, with different desires and goals in life. In my case, I had a clear mission, vision, purpose, and goal in real estate. Achieving my goal of producing 100 transactions per year was part of it. It was one way of my measuring my ability to be the best I could be in real estate.

Your goals may be different than my goals. That's the beauty of the world we live in. However, one of the challenges we have in life is what happens when someone who has a goal to produce 100 transactions a year seeks guidance from someone whose goals and aspirations are not in alignment with theirs. That person may provide us with partial, inaccurate, or biased information, and if we take it at face value we may begin to believe it as "the truth." We then record "the truth" in our subconscious in the form of beliefs. Once we deem it to be true, we begin to carry out those beliefs in the form of our habits and attitudes.

Our subconscious performs two important functions: control of our habits and control of our attitudes. Let's look at what habits and attitudes are and see why they can be so difficult to change. As the world changes around us, it becomes extremely important to discard old obsolete habits and attitudes and replace them with more useful ones.

Our habits and attitudes are directly related to the subconscious beliefs that we hold about ourselves and the world around us.

Habits. Our habits are behaviors that have been repeated often enough to be effortless and automatic. They are second-nature patterns we possess. Habits enable us to move smoothly through life. They also allow us to do certain things without thinking about them. Once we learn how or develop the habit pattern, we go through our normal daily practice and do countless things as a matter of routine.

Most of our habitual behavior is good for us; it enables us to function efficiently. However, some habits stored on the subconscious level can create obstacles or barriers when we seek to stay focused on our goals or make changes in our lives to become more aligned with our mission, vision, purpose, goals, and values. We find ourselves using old habit patterns when trying to deal with new experiences and challenges. These comfortable yet obsolete habit patterns can sometimes hinder our ability to achieve our goals.

Our habits stop being good and useful for us at that point when change enters the picture. Once we establish our aims or new aims, if our steps, needs, and goals to realize them require that we develop new habit patterns to successfully achieve them, we have to make a decision to make changes in those areas of our lives. Once we've made that decision, we will need to take proactive steps to properly align our habits with our aims.

These days, change is becoming more of an everyday occurrence, thanks in part to the world's population's becoming more diverse and rapidly developing new technologies. The way we used to think and behave may not work in this changing world today.

The same can be said for when we set a goal as part of pursuing our vision. If our goals cause us to venture into new territory, like seeking to transition from one profession to another or increasing our personal income, and we've been trying to make the change without much success, we should consider what habit patterns we would need to change to bring our habits in alignment with our mission, vision, purpose, goals, and values. The habit patterns we have gotten used to in life may not enable us to be most effective and efficient in pursuing our aims.

For many people, changing habits is traumatic. Some of us seek to avoid, deny, or resist change for as long as possible. But the more we resist, the harder things become for us. Our habits seem to be cast in stone, and some of us may even blame others for the anxiety and resentment we feel. The good news is that habits can be changed. Taking steps to change our habits to reflect the alignment of our mission, vision, purpose, goals, and values will assist us in remaining focused on our goals while in the storm.

Attitudes. Attitudes are similar to habits in that they, too, are sometimes difficult to change. An attitude is a direction in which we lean. It's an emotional response to a perception that we have learned over time. The response can be neutral, positive, or negative. Positive doesn't always mean good, and negative doesn't necessarily mean bad. However, once we set a goal, if we lean toward it, our attitude is thought to be positive; if we lean away from it, our attitude is considered to be negative.

We aren't born with our attitudes — we learn them over time. They start out on the conscious level and through repetition they move to the subconscious level.

Our habits and attitudes reflect our subconscious beliefs about who we perceive ourselves to be and our expectation of others. When we change those beliefs, our habits and attitudes change easily, effortlessly, and in a natural, free-flowing way.

Like our habits, many of our attitudes are good and useful, up to the point when change enters the picture. After establishing our mission, vision, purpose, goals, and values, if the steps, needs, and goals to realize our vision require that we change our attitudes in certain areas to successfully complete the journey, we must commit to making those changes. Once we make that decision, we must take steps to properly align our attitudes with our mission, vision, purpose, goals, and values.

The creative subconscious is the part of our mind that controls our behavior. The difference between the subconscious and the creative subconscious is that the subconscious creates the picture that we know ourselves to be, and the creative subconscious acts on that picture.

The creative subconscious has three primary functions:

- First, it causes us to act like the person we know ourselves to be; it maintains our self-image. To maintain sanity, we must act like the subconscious picture we hold of ourselves.

- Second, the creative subconscious creatively solves problems. The problems are solved in a natural, free-flowing manner.

- Third, the creative subconscious provides energy and drive. When it senses a problem or obstacle standing in the way of our goal, it provides great drive, energy, and motivation to find answers and a solution.

So, if we're in sales and we don't like receiving phone calls at home or at the office or if we fear being rejected by the person we're calling because the first time we think the person we've called replied in a rude manner, our creative subconscious will go to work to solve the problem.

We will talk more about the creative subconscious in the next chapter; however, for now know that one function of the creative subconscious is to solve the conflict that occurs when the image we have of ourselves does not match events in our external environment. This conflict is not all bad; in some cases, the conflict may be constructive.

In fact, creating this kind of challenge for ourselves can be a good thing. The clearer our mission, vision, purpose, goals, and values become to us, the more discontented we will be with our current reality. And our creative subconscious will go to work searching for ways to resolve the conflict. At the same time, we're adjusting our subconscious beliefs about who we know ourselves to be and what we can do to change that self-image. We're creating tremendous drive and energy to achieve our goals and make the changes in our lives we desire. This energy can greatly assist us in making necessary changes to enable us to remain focused on our aims, even when we are caught in a storm.

CHAPTER 23

ALIGN EXPECTATIONS WITH AIMS

As we look deeper into how we naturally respond when our expectations are not met, we realize there are a number of factors that weigh in on why and how we respond the way we do when our expectations are not met in life. These range from our life experiences, to our beliefs, habit patterns, attitudes, and expectations.

When I think back on why I had a fear of making sales calls, it was in part because of what I perceived as some negative experiences I had had with both making and receiving phone calls at home in my life. If we have this fear, we can probably look back in our lives to an event that contributed to the beliefs we hold today in those areas.

If someone said to us "You're not good at something" and we fell short or failed at accomplishing that task, we might translate that comment into a belief that we "lack what it takes" to succeed. As a result, this becomes "the truth" in our eyes, based on how we view the world. Based on this truth as we believe it or perceive it to be, we go around living our lives based on those beliefs and "truths."

When we explore where many of the beliefs we hold today came from, we may discover that much of the knowledge we use to determine "the truth" in our lives comes from generalities we have drawn from our life experiences and the way we have been conditioned to think. So, an important question to consistently ask ourselves is: "Where do the beliefs I hold come from?" This is especially important if those beliefs are not properly aligned with our aims in life.

This is an important question to ask and answer because some generalities we make in life are based on limited experience, limited information, misrepresentation, or our perception of "the truth."

Based on the power of our beliefs, we may look for information to validate what we perceive to be the truth. We become selective in searching for information that will reinforce our beliefs. This persistence is evident when we have conflicting beliefs or attitudes such as "I know I need to make sales calls in order to achieve my sales goals; however, I have a fear of rejection when I make them."

When we experience such a conflict we tend to be influenced in our search by the kind of information that will validate our strongest beliefs. Our approach might become so biased that it leads to a partial or inaccurate view of the facts. We might become so persistent in our pursuit of what we believe to be the truth that we lose track of our goal.

Another aspect that increases the persistence with which we pursue what we deem to be the truth is the self-fulfilling prophecy. We may act on our beliefs in such a way that we bring about the expected results we're seeking. For example, salespeople who think that the person on the other end of the call will be rude to them may act in a manner that causes them to be hesitant in speaking to the person during the call, even though the person on the other end of the line may be polite. These salespeople are acting in a way consistent with their expectations.

Expectations influence our behavior in such a way as to validate them. For example, in major league baseball, managers are highly paid to make daily decisions to put their team in the best position for success. They will use information gathered by their scouting department to assist them in their decision-making process.

Managers have access to all sorts of information on every single player, all the way down to how one performs against the other. When making decisions, they will almost always go with the decision that will give them the greatest odds of success based on the information they have available to them. They believe this step will put them and their team in the best position for success.

That's why late in a baseball game the manager will bring in a right-handed relief pitcher to face a right-handed batter. The information they're using based on prior experience indicates that right-handed pitchers have a greater opportunity of success in scoring an "out" for their team than does a left-handed pitcher in that situation. Therefore, a decision is almost always made to go with the right-handed pitcher. In their opinion, they believe they are being paid to take this step to put the team in the best position for success.

When we hold certain beliefs, such as with the baseball manager, we can take steps daily moving us closer to the attainment of our goals in life, even though we will run into twists, turns, and roadblocks along the way.

On the flip side, we often allow certain experiences in our lives to override substantial amounts of statistical information. For example, a salesperson may read about a survey of 5,000 sales calls, indicating that people are okay with receiving sales calls as long as the caller is courteous, but they may disregard that important information when a friend or coworker says, "I received a call from a salesperson that interrupted our family time, and I did not like it."

Therefore, when we hold certain beliefs that may not be in alignment with our aims, negative comments may hinder our ability to consistently take steps to move closer to achieving those goals on a daily basis. In that case we must work diligently to take steps to properly align our "expectations" with our aims in life.

Expectations play a vital role in all our lives. Aligning expectations with our aims can be a difficult task for some of us because of how we have learned to think and how we see the world.

As we have previously pointed out, if we hold obsolete or mistaken beliefs based on the way we have been conditioned to think, we will behave as if they were true. If the comments we hear from others are based on obsolete or mistaken beliefs or the way we have been conditioned to think and we take them out of context or at face value, we behave as if they were true. We act not in accordance with the objective truth but with the truth as we believe it or perceive it to be.

Our beliefs possess enormous power. Our thoughts about what is true through our vision help guide our behavior. Based on how our subconscious works, any behavior that we seek that conflicts with our beliefs tends to quickly disappear. Our creative subconscious ensures that we act the way we know ourselves to be.

When we behave in ways that do not reflect the person we know ourselves to be, our creative subconscious goes to work to correct the picture. It corrects the "mistake" by changing our behavior back to fit our self-image — the dominant picture we have of ourselves. Even if we are trying to change for the better, if our subconscious believes that "better" is not like our thoughts and behavior, it will automatically ensure that our efforts to change fail. That's why we begin the process of change on the inside with our subconscious.

Often our beliefs have much more to do with other people's opinions than with the real truth. Remember the conditioning process that we all have gone through to develop the beliefs, habits, and attitudes we hold today. Be aware that many of our opinions about ourselves and others may be based on limited information or limited thinking.

Our beliefs possess enormous power. Basically, our thoughts about what is true through our eyes as a result of our conditioning help guide our behavior. Based on how our subconscious works, any behavior that we seek that conflicts with our beliefs tends to quickly disappear. The part of our mind that helps achieve this function is our creative subconscious, which assures that we act the way we know ourselves to be.

When we behave in ways that do not reflect the person we know ourselves to be, our creative subconscious goes to work to correct the picture. It corrects the "mistake" by changing our behavior back to fit our self-image — the dominant picture we have of ourselves. That's why "trying harder" doesn't always work. If our deepest beliefs about ourselves are that we can't succeed or that we don't deserve to succeed, we will not succeed no matter how hard we try. Our creative subconscious will find a way to make sure we fail in our efforts to succeed. Once we change our dominant internal picture of ourselves to that of a successful person, our efforts to make a change for the better will begin to pay off.

Once again, lasting change starts on the inside. If we're trying to make the changes necessary to achieve our goals, we must first change the way we think in certain areas and properly align our expectations with our aims. Behind everything we do is a thought. Every behavior is motivated by a belief, and every action is prompted by an attitude. If we desire to stay focused on our goals and to change our lives for the better, we must start first internally by aligning our thoughts and beliefs with what we really want in life.

Realizing our goals and becoming the person we desire to become begins with a decision to grow personally. This is where I draw on my life experiences from sports. As a former professional athlete, it was our team's desire to be the best in the world in our sport. In order to achieve that goal, we had to work at it.

Elite world-class athletes wake up each day and ask themselves, "How can I be better today than yesterday and how can I be better tomorrow than today?" This requires ongoing personal and professional growth and development as well as consistent skill development to be the best we can be. The same process will enable us to remain focused on our goals despite the obstacles we encounter.

Being able to remain focused on our goals, even in the eye of a storm, does not mean we're going to be perfect. It does not mean we're going to have success every day. There are simply going to be some days when, no matter what we do, it's not going to be our day. What we must do on those days is to remain focused on consistently and skillfully practicing the basic fundamentals of our profession, despite encountering obstacles or barriers along the way.

As previously mentioned, when we went to training camp in football each year, we knew we might lose 25% to 40% of our games that year and still have an opportunity to achieve our ultimate goal of winning the Super Bowl. That meant we were going to have some bad days, days when things were not going to go well for us. The same applies to us in our everyday lives. There are days when things are not going to go our way. The question is how do we manage our expectations on those days, or in some cases for longer periods of time, when things are not falling into place for us?

One of the most significant things I learned from playing sports revolved around the importance of properly aligning our expectations with our aims in life. And learning how to be the best we can be each day, especially when things are going badly. And that includes learning that being the best we can be every day does not mean we're going to win or meet our expectations every day. This is especially the case if we're going against strong competition or pursing a huge goal. The bigger the goal or the greater the competition, the greater the need for us to learn how to manage our expectations when things are not turning out well for us.

Regardless of what space we operate in, managing expectations is about applying knowledge, wisdom, skills, character traits, and other valuable traits we possess when we need to apply them.

It's about understanding and consistently and skillfully practicing the basic fundamentals of whatever space we operate in. This is especially true when we encounter negative circumstances in life, things not going as planned, or negative comments we hear from others. These are success patterns practiced by champions.

Being a champion is not about being perfect. It's about successfully managing expectations in a manner that will enable that player or person to remain focused on taking steps to accomplish his or her goals in life, one step at a time.

Being a champion is about having faith and confidence so that when we confidently and skillfully practice the basic fundamentals in whatever space we operate in, we move one step closer to achieving our goals in life.

Aligning our expectations with our aims in life is about being on a permanent search for the best way to confidentially and skillfully take steps daily to put ourselves in the best position to achieve our goals. And to do so knowing that when we lay our heads down on our pillow each night, we can do so with inner peace, self-satisfaction, and self-fulfillment knowing that we've given it the very best we had to offer.

CHAPTER 24

CONCENTRATE ON YOUR CIRCLE OF FOCUS

Early in my NFL career, I became interested in tennis, so much so that I decided to begin playing the game recreationally.

When I first began playing the sport, naturally I was not very good. This was never more evident than when I played against really experienced tennis players. Although I was an exceptional athlete, my athleticism was no match for the advanced tennis players I was competing against.

After soundly getting my butt kicked over and over again, I decided to hire a tennis coach. My goal was to become as fundamentally sound in tennis as I was in football. I wanted to be the best I could be in the sport. I knew that would be a difficult task, since I started playing football in the 7th grade, and I had just started tennis.

When I first began working with my tennis coach, the first step he took was to begin teaching me about the basic fundamentals and the associated terminology for the sport. This was an important step because he worked with me to identify what was going to be in the center of my circle of focus in tennis. We will talk more about our circle of focus later in the chapter, but just be aware that by my coach taking this step, it moved me closer to achieving my goals in tennis, although I did not realize it at the time.

In football, I thoroughly understood the fundamentals of the game. Over the years, I had spent many hours and days perfecting my skills, and I could confidentially and skillfully execute them. In tennis, I was literally just learning the basics of the game.

Once we moved to practicing on the tennis court, my coach began working with me on the basic shots of the game. These included a topspin forehand, a topspin backhand, a flat first serve, a kick second serve, a forehand and backhand volley, and both a forehand and backhand return of serve. I was familiar with many of these shots from watching the pro tennis tournaments on TV. What I didn't realize was how hard it was to consistently hit those shots on the court until I began practicing them with my tennis coach.

I realized I had a lot of work ahead of me to achieve my goals in tennis. To get where I wanted to get, it was going to require my complete focus and a real commitment on my behalf to practice the various tennis shots of the game often and consistently. This was never more evident than when I interacted with some of the tennis players, who had been playing tennis as long as I had been playing football. They had put in a lot of time crafting their skills, and it showed in their confidence on the court.

Tennis players who had been playing the game for a long time had hit millions of balls during their careers. That's why they were as good as they were. I knew I needed practice time. And if I was going to be the best I could be in the sport, I needed that practice time to be on par with the focus and intensity I was accustomed to in football.

This was early in my NFL career, and I knew I could only focus on tennis during the off season. Therefore, I committed to incorporate my tennis practice schedule during the off season around my football training. I used tennis as a means of staying active and working on my quickness and reflexes. The more active I became in the sport, the more I loved it.

This is when I started to think about what did I, as a football player, have in common with tennis players that I could use to enhance my performance in the sport? To further validate what I was looking for, I thought of what football and tennis players might have in common with players from other sports, such as basketball, volleyball, or baseball. The conclusion I arrived at was that there was a common denominator of the ability to narrow our focus to improve our effectiveness as player.

In all aspects of life, we see ourselves as being good but not perfect at something, such as having a good backhand in tennis but not being so strong on the forehand side. That was my case. The moment my opponents made this discovery, the best players narrowed their focus and they consistently hit the ball to my weaker side, my forehand, in an attempt to gain an advantage. Conversely, they worked to get balls returned to them to their more skillful side, whether it was their forehand or backhand.

Players in all sports take similar steps. We did it in football, where we narrowed our focus to attack our opponent's weakness and played to our strengths. We managed our weaknesses and capitalized on our strengths.

One of the first things I realized when I first started playing tennis was that I had the potential to be a good player in the sport. The one thing I lacked was all the hours of practice time the other tennis players had under their belt. They were practicing tennis growing up when I was practicing football.

I worked diligently early in my tennis career to develop the confidence and skills to be as fundamentally sound in tennis as I was in football. As I continued to work in this area, I became more aware of my strengths and weaknesses in the sport. As part of the process, I learned how to narrow my focus in a way to play to my strengths and manage my weaknesses, while continuing to work on improving my overall all-around game. Taking this step enabled me to be able to utilize more of my God-given potential in the sport. I ultimately went on to play on the pro-amateur celebrity tennis tour. I had an opportunity to play with and against some of the world's top tennis players in doubles. Today, it's one of my goals to remain active as one of the top tennis players in my age group.

What can we all learn from highly effective people across all sectors of society? Well, it's their ability to narrow their focus and play to their strengths while working diligently on improving their weaknesses without losing sight of the big picture. That enables them to increase their focus and utilize more of their God-given gifts and talents.

What might prevent us from utilizing a similar approach? One is a lack of focus in the right areas of our lives. We each have a wide range of areas we can focus on in life: our health, our family, our marriage, our children, our work, the sport we play, our problems, the economy.

Over some areas, we have either direct or indirect control. But over other areas, we have little or no control. Highly effective people invest their time, effort, and energy on things over which they have direct or indirect control, and they lock out those things over which they have no control. Like the great tennis and football players, they select an area they have control of and that's what they focus on.

In our lives, there are things which we have direct or indirect control of and others over which we have no control. Highly effective people separate those things over which they have no specific control by creating a circle of focus. Inside the circle, they place those things they have either direct or indirect control over and that's where they focus their time, effort, and energy. They place those things over which they have no control outside their circle of focus in their area of no control.

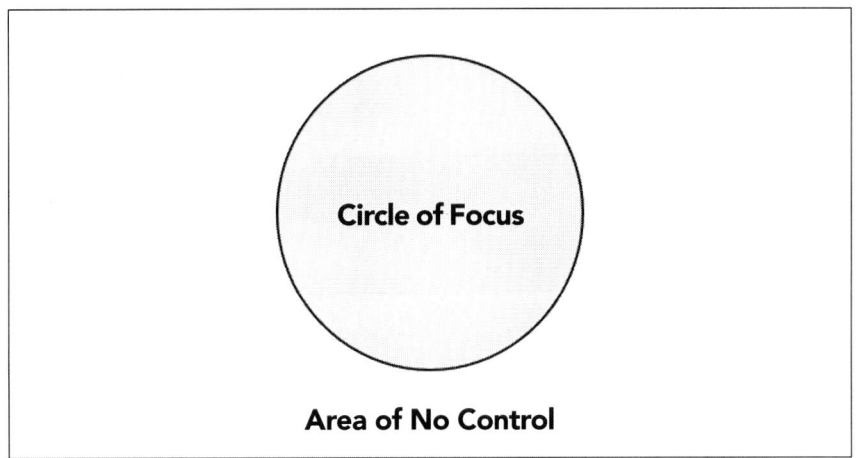

Circle of Focus

Area of No Control

By determining which of these two areas we are to focus on, especially when we encounter twists, turns, and roadblocks, we will be able to move closer to achieving our goals in life. Highly effective people focus their efforts inside their circle of focus when they find themselves in the midst of a storm. They proactively work on those things they can do something about.

Conversely, those of us who waste our time and energy on things over which we have no control often find ourselves emotionally reacting and focusing on the storms in our lives. We focus on circumstances over which we have no control. Our focus may result in accusing others for the storms. The negative energy generated by our misplaced focus of our time, effort, and energy, combined with neglect in the areas we can do something about, causes us to lose our focus on our goals.

By narrowing our focus without losing site of the big picture, the problems we face usually fall in one of three areas: *direct control*, or problems involving our own behavior; *indirect control*, or problems involving other people's behavior; or *no control*, that is, things we can do nothing about, such as our past.

Working on our beliefs, habits, attitudes, and expectations can assist us in solving many of our direct control problems. These problems fall within our circle of focus.

We can effectively address indirect control problems that involve other people's behavior by changing the way we deal with them. Most of us try reasoning to deal with these problems. If that doesn't work, we may fight or escape the problem by running away.

Although we can't control the behavior of others in our lives, we can control our reaction to their behavior; hence, indirect control problems are placed inside our circle of focus.

Dealing with no control problems involves learning to genuinely accept them, whether we like them or not. Although we can't control these problems, we can control how we respond to them. If it's something we can't do anything about, we will need to "let it go." With this approach, we do not allow these problems to control us. They are outside our circle of focus and in our area of no control.

Highly effective people make a habit of not empowering those things in their lives that they have no control over. When they encounter twists, turns, and roadblocks in life, they ask themselves, "Can I do anything about these circumstances or situation?" If the answer is no, then the best thing to do is not to worry about them because they can't control the situation in any case.

When you evaluate the performances of highly effective people in storms, you recognize that one key to their success is their ability to focus their time, efforts, and energies on things they can control. One of the primary reasons why they are able to remain focused is their ability to "separate emotion from logic" while in the storm.

Emotions drive many of the decisions we make in life. If we feel uncomfortable in a particular situation, we tend to shy away from the situation or retreat back to an area in which we feel more comfortable. The situation can bring about certain emotions in the form of stress and anxiety within us. Those emotions can cause us to make decisions that may not be in alignment with our aims in life.

Another area in which our emotions can test us is when we are confronted with a situation where something we believe to be true is violated. When our beliefs and the situation we find ourselves in don't match, we experience a certain set of emotions. Depending on what drives us, we can become overwhelmed with the situation as a result of our emotions.

For example, we can become so overwhelmed by frustration and anger that these emotions lead us to making decisions that are not in alignment with our mission, vision, purpose, goals, and values. These improper reactions and behaviors hinder our ability to remain focused on our goals.

When we find ourselves in a storm, we must keep in mind that it may not be the circumstance that is causing the problem; it may be some of our subconscious beliefs. Where we place our focus while in the storm may be causing the problem. Tough circumstances just bring those subconscious beliefs to the surface. Often our reactions may have more to do with those beliefs and where we are placing our focus than the actual circumstances.

Usually our emotions operate at their peak during storms. The better we manage our emotions while in the midst of a storm in our lives, the better we'll remain focused on our mission, vision, purpose, goals, and values.

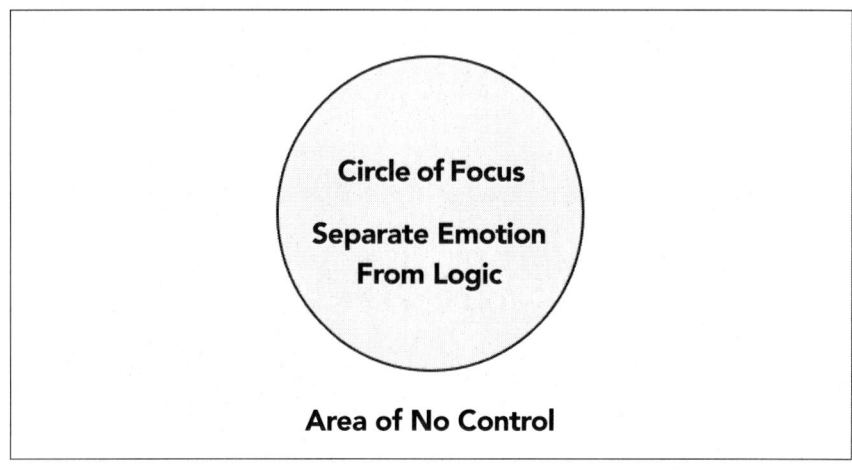

Area of No Control

Highly effective people have an exceptional way of separating emotion from logic when dealing with those things that fall within their "circle of focus."

I encourage you to take this approach and not allow anyone or anything to have so much control over you that it affects the way you live your life or conduct your business. If you have control of something, "lock-on" to it; if you do not have control of it, "lock it out." Focus your time and energies only on things that you can control.

In other words, if you do not have control over something, I encourage you not to worry about it. Don't let it affect you. When dealing with no-control problem areas, what you "lock-on" to and "lock-out" is key, along with how quickly you adapt to the unfamiliar surroundings. The example is my going from the football field to the tennis court. I have no control over where my opponent hits the ball, so I "lock-on" to where and how I hit the ball in return, whether it is from my stronger backhand or weaker forehand side. I can only control the things that I am able to control.

Whether a problem is *direct, indirect,* or *no control,* we can seek a solution based on where we choose to focus our time, efforts, and energy. In choosing the correct response to the storms in our lives, we can positively affect the situation we find ourselves in. Once we determine what's inside our "circle of focus," we can be accountable for our reaction to the storms in our lives. Where we focus our time, effort, and energy is a key part of that process. This enables us to remain focused on our goals, even when we're in the middle of a storm in life.

SECTION

6

WORKING FROM INSIDE OUT

Highly effective people have a unique way of controlling their self-talk, especially when they encounter the normal twists, turns, and roadblocks we all run into while pursuing our goals in life. They specifically know how to remain focused on their mission, vision, purpose, goals, and values when they encounter difficult circumstances, things not going as planned, or negative comments they hear from others. Taking these steps will continue to lead us toward attainment of our goals.

CHAPTER 25

BE CAREFUL WHAT YOU SAY TO YOURSELF

If we think back in our lives, we can probably think of someone who told us we were not good at something and their comments remain with us today. It may have been our parents, a teacher, a coach, our spouse, or maybe our boss who shared their negative opinions about us, and for some reason it continues to stay with us. If similar comments are made to us today, we start repeating them in our minds, especially if we believe they may be consistent with an opinion we have of ourselves.

When we set a goal and head out to achieve it, we know we will run into obstacles and barriers along the way. That's especially the case when we transition to the next phase of our lives or to a new space. If some of the normal twists, turns, and roadblocks we run into along the way are consistent with the comments we've heard before that are not aligned with our aims in life, they may hinder our ability to be the best we can be.

When I first started selling real estate, I was not very good at it, and I saw myself that way. When I first started playing tennis, I was not very good at that either. Conversely, I felt like I was one of the best in the world in football, and that's how I saw myself.

Compare that to my early days in real estate and tennis. I was not very good at either. That was simply because I had not had ample time to work to become better, like many of the other seasoned agents in real estate or the players who had been playing tennis for years. It had nothing to do with my potential to excel in either one. I lacked the time and experience spent conducting real estate activities that some of the others in the business had accumulated, and I did not have the practice and game experience the other tennis players had under their belt in the sport.

When I first started selling real estate and playing tennis, there were three things I had to guard against in each space as related to how I talked to myself. These included circumstances, things not going as planned, and negative comments I heard from others. I encountered each of these obstacles while pursuing my goals in both real estate and tennis. When I ran into obstacles, it was important for me to be careful in what I said to myself.

Here's the reason why. Our thought patterns play a role in creating and maintaining our self-image by the way we talk to ourselves. These silent conversations are called self-talk. They are the little voices we hear talking to us in our head. They often take the form of thoughts —thoughts about our activities, feelings, and experiences. These thoughts trigger pictures that cause feelings or emotions in us. Our self-talk helps shape and form our self-image.

As a professional athlete, I saw myself as being one of the best at my position in the National Football League. That was the image I had of myself as a player. When I ran into storms as an NFL player, I utilized positive self-talk daily to affirm and enhance my beliefs.

Unfortunately, as a real estate professional, it was just the opposite. I often beat myself up with negative self-talk, especially when things did not go as planned or when I heard negative comments from others that were consistent with the negative thoughts I was thinking about myself. I knew that if I truly desired to achieve my real estate goals, I must first change my beliefs about myself as a real estate professional. In order to successfully accomplish this goal, I knew I had to change my self-talk to be more in alignment with my real estate goals.

Our beliefs influence our daily behavior. And our behavior plays a major role in determining our results and the success we can expect to experience in life. Our self-talk can lead us to happiness and success. But it can hinder us as well.

The bigger the goals are that we pursue, the greater the possibility of us running into twists, turns, and roadblocks along the way. Also, the bigger the goals, the greater the possibility of us hearing negative comments that are not aligned with our goals in life. This was certainly the case early in my tennis career. I heard over and over again that I had a weak forehand or a weak second serve. And of course, when I went on the court and my forehand or second serve was off, I frequently validated those comments in my mind with my self-talk.

Something else to think about is what happens when other people put us down or build us up with what they say to us? Does their talk have the same impact as what we say to ourselves? Yes, if we buy into it and accept it as the truth. But if it's negative and we reject what another person has to say about us, their opinion won't have an impact on us. However, we have to truly reject it knowing the impact it can have on us and our self-image

If what others say is negative, we must counter it with a positive truth of our own. We don't have to do it out loud, but we need to counteract it. No one can tear us down but ourselves. But that's also the bad news if we have the habit of tearing ourselves down.

Successful people are in the habit of seeing the best in themselves and affirming it with their thoughts and words. They do so whether they're a professional football player, new in real estate sales, or just starting to play tennis. They're not bragging;

they are building themselves up by confirming their own ability and potential.

It was important for me to transfer my positive self-talk from football to both real estate and tennis, although it was going to be a struggle for me. I knew that the more I affirmed and confirmed my strengths, the stronger I would be. And the more we affirm our ability to learn and grow the more learning and growing we will do and thereby remain focused on our aims in life.

Changing my self-talk played a vital role in changing my beliefs to be more in alignment with my aims in real estate. It also played a key role in changing my beliefs to be more in alignment with my goals in tennis. Taking both steps enabled me to move closer to achieving my overall mission, vision, purpose, and goals in life, and I didn't even realize it at that time.

One of my goals as a real estate professional and tennis player was to align my activities and behavior in both areas with the success patterns I was accustomed to in football. In addition to controlling my self-talk, another step I took to build my self-image as a real estate professional and tennis player was to affirm my goals daily. As a pro football player, I used these techniques faithfully.

Taking these steps are key. That's because positive affirmation helps us make changes in the areas we desire from the inside out starting with our subconscious beliefs. When we seek to align our behavior with our aims, if we try to change from the outside in, we may struggle to maintain the new behavior. However, if we work from the inside out, by changing our subconscious beliefs first to be aligned with our desired behavior we will experience lasting change and greater use of our full potential.

Daily, we affirm things in our mind: "I am good at that." "I am not good at that." "I am a patient person." "I am an impatient person." These affirmations can impact our lives if we accept them as the truth, particularly since an affirmation is merely a statement of our personal truth.

Affirmations are potent. The technique of using positive affirmations and visualization is taught to world-class athletes and used by other highly effective people — from doctors, surgeons, and airline pilots to salespeople and entertainers.

One reason why positive or negative affirmations have such an impact on our belief system is because our subconscious can't tell the difference between something intensely imagined and a real experience. That's why dreams feel so real to us.

Affirmations are powerful statements that can deeply affect our subconscious mind. Because our subconscious accepts anything we intensely imagine as reality, visualizing and affirming our goals empowers us to attain them. We can develop the habit of affirming the changes we're seeking and visualizing ourselves in the new behavior we desire. When done consistently and correctly, this process will assist us in removing some of the stress and pushback that accompanies our change efforts. It's a very effective way to create change from the inside out.

Because of the potential impact of affirmations, for better or for worse, we must learn how to write affirmations correctly. This will assist us in creating powerful visual images that bring about the right pictures and emotions when we are reading and thinking about our affirmations. This will also assist us in simulating the desired outcome we are pursuing.

When we practice using positive affirmations and visualization regularly, we are experiencing through vivid, detailed mental pictures exactly what we want to happen to us and how we desire to behave. We are simulating the experience we desire. The more we repeat the affirmation with the right spirit of intent, the greater impact it will have on our subconscious. The more twists, turns, and roadblocks we run into while we're in pursuit of our goals, the greater the need to repeat the affirmations with the right spirit of intent.

As we pursue our goals, we will encounter adverse circumstances, things will not go as planned, and we will hear negative comments from others that are not aligned with our aims. This is when the use of good sound positive affirmations, written properly, will assist us in applying our knowledge and wisdom when we need to when we encounter obstacles or barriers in life. They will assist us in tapping into our healthy competitive spirit to bring true meaning to the character words like courage, persistence, patience, resiliency, and others as needed at the appropriate time to enable us to remain focused on our goals when we encounter obstacles along the way.

The more I was able to take the steps as a real estate professional and in tennis that I was accustomed to accelerating my progress as a professional athlete in football, the more aligned my behavior became with my goals and vision in real estate and tennis. The more I controlled my self-talk and affirmed my goals daily, the more my self-image changed from that of a pro football player in a business suit to that of a real estate professional who played pro football. This helped bring about a dramatic change in the results I began to experience in the real estate industry as I moved closer to realizing my real estate goals. I went on to hit my goal of producing 100 closed transactions a year in real estate. The same thing transpired in tennis. I went on to become one of the best pro-amateur celebrity tennis players in the country.

When our affirmations are written correctly and when we make this process a part of our daily routine, we'll find ourselves using much more of our full potential. We'll see ourselves growing and changing in positive ways because positive affirmations give us a vivid mental experience of success. When we create this successful experience over and over again, it becomes assimilated into our self- image. It becomes "part of us" to behave that way. This process enables us to move one step closer to achieving our goals in life.

CHAPTER 26

TURNING DREAMS INTO REALITY

Whenever you transition to a new job, career, profession, or any new space in general, I encourage you to take two steps. The first is to ask the leader in charge what are the core basic fundamental activities that if practiced confidently and skillfully will put you in the best position for success in achieving your goals? Next, ask them what skills that if practiced confidently and carefully on a daily basis will put you in best position to perform the fundamental activities?

When positive affirmations are written correctly, and we understand and confidently and skillfully practice the basic fundamentals of whatever space we operate in, we move closer to achieving our goals in life. When we make this process a part of our daily routine, we'll find ourselves using much more of our full potential. We'll see ourselves growing and changing in positive ways.

When we create these successful experiences over and over again, in our minds and in reality, they become assimilated into our self-image. It becomes "like us" to behave that way. When our mission, vision, purpose, goals, and values are properly aligned and our affirmations are written and used correctly, our actions move us closer to achieving our goals in life. However, these steps and processes will not necessarily make the journey any easier. It's still going to be hard, but we will overcome it.

On a cold night in January, Rachel Swearingen and her friend Alex Ruiz, both in their early twenties at the time, sat in their car and contemplated their futures. They discussed what dreams and aspirations were tucked away in their hearts that had not yet seen the light. Rachel asked Alex what she was dreaming about and she softly whispered, "I'm dreaming of traveling the world and filming what God is doing."

Rewind to a couple of months earlier when their pastor at their local church was telling them about a revival he was hearing about all over the world. People were coming to know Jesus, being healed, and spreading the gospel in their villages around the world.

The night they were sitting in Rachel's car talking about Alex's dream, they decided they could be the ones to film what God was doing around the world. They were hearing of the deep-seated religious movement taking place in countries such as Mongolia, India, Brazil, and other places, and they decided that they wanted to see what they were hearing about.

Rachel and Alex talked about their generation and how they wanted to see things they were hearing about close up. They were visual in picturing the things they wanted to see. They decided they needed to capture what God was doing around the world through film and show people the powerful stories they had been hearing about.

They brainstormed their idea and sought counsel on whether or not they could accomplish it. Alex was a film major at Colorado State University and had been working as a reporter for the last couple of years. Rachel was still a communication major at Colorado State University. She had never even held a camera or filmed anything.

Despite their inadequacies, the two young ladies felt like they were on a mission and were determined to pursue their dream. They got the drawing board out and started brainstorming. They wanted to leave at the beginning of June of that year so they knew they had 12 weeks in which to raise the funds and figure out the route they wanted to travel the world. They wanted to travel to different cultures to see what God looked like to different groups of people.

And although the idea sounded totally unrealistic and even unsafe to many people, they began reaching out to missionaries, friends of missionaries, pastors, family members, pretty much anyone they knew who they felt might know someone who lived overseas. They were searching for people who were seeing the powerful movement of God they were searching for. By taking this step, they were closer to bringing their dreams to life.

They decided to start in Mongolia, head to Lebanon, continue to England, Dubai, India, Uganda, and South Africa, and end in San Diego.

They started raising funds by hosting a small gathering in Rachel's backyard where they created a video that highlighted their mission and shared their master plan in a clear and exciting way. They raised about $600 at this first gathering. They had a long way to go; however, they were much closer to achieving their goals but didn't realize it at the moment because their dream still appeared so far away.

They posted their video on social media and started sharing it with people all around the U.S. They called pastors, churches, friends, families, people they had never met. They showed their video to thousands of people, hoping that they would catch onto their vision.

They next decided to go to Seattle to meet with a producer of Christian films. He agreed to meet with them and gave them strategies on how to create a successful movie. They went to Waco several times and met with a church which had a huge planning movement. They asked for their connections, resources, and financial support.

Slowly but surely, they consistently, confidentially, and skillfully practiced the necessary fundamental activities to raise enough money to purchase their first couple of tickets. In the beginning of June, they packed their bags, purchased all the camera gear they needed, and they were off!

They started in Mongolia and barely ate because they didn't want to spend their money poorly. They ate Kentucky Fried Chicken once a day and would splurge on a coffee! But they felt the Lord was faithful and true enough so that through their consistent, skillful, and fundamentally sound fundraising activities, the funds kept coming.

They traveled through the hills of Mongolia, the mountains of Lebanon, and the cities of England, and when they got to India they realized they didn't have enough money to go on to Uganda. Like most of us might in a situation like that, they started to panic a little bit and doubt started to creep in about the success of their entire mission and goal. They started asking themselves, "What are we doing?" "Was this even going to work?" "Was this a good idea?"

Naturally, most of us would think and feel that way based on the circumstances they found themselves in. This was especially true because they felt they had planned things out well. However, what happened to them may occur to many of us when we set a huge goal and set out to accomplish it. There are going to be times when things are not going to go as planned. This was certainly the case with these two young ladies.

This is when Rachel remembered something she felt the Lord had laid on her heart before she left. She felt He told her that money was going to be to them like Manna was to the Israelis in the old testament. She felt they were going to get exactly what they needed, exactly when they need it. And they did! The next morning, they woke up and someone had given them exactly what they needed to go on to Uganda.

In each country they visited they produced a short video to highlight their time there. They did this so that people could have a better understanding of what they were doing. They also took that step to continue marketing their idea so they could continue raising funds. Today, these two young women are on to the next phase of their lives. The dreams they so vividly visualized had become a reality.

It took a lot of confidence, faith, and humility for them to ask for help to pursue a dream that many probably thought was crazy. I know from my work in leading World Class Coaches how hard it must have been for Rachel and Alex to bring their dreams to reality.

Most of all, I know how hard it must have been for them to know that they were in need of assistance from the community to buy into their mission when many people may have thought they were crazy. Many people also thought it was unsafe for two young women to travel on such a dangerous mission. However, in the final analysis, it was beautiful to see the effect of those people who believed in their mission and vision and helped them make their dreams become reality.

CHAPTER 27

WHEN DREAMS BECOME REALITY - EXPAND YOUR COMFORT ZONE

When dreams become reality, the question is what's next? Well we know goal-setting is an ongoing process. There's a need to consistently set new goals once we achieve our existing ones. If we fail to take this step, we can easily lose our drive and motivation.

But there's another step we will need to take to put ourselves in the best position to use more of our full potential and achieve more of our aims in life. We will need to expand our comfort zone. The bigger our goals are, the more likely we may feel uncomfortable in the new environment we find ourselves in once we achieve our goals. That's the case, although the goal is precisely what we desire in life. This is a sign that we're out of our comfort zone.

As previously mentioned, I played on the varsity in football as a freshman in high school. I started as a defensive back. I recall that in my first game my coach put me back to return a punt. If you're not familiar with punting or kickoffs in football, that's when one team kicks the ball to their opponents at various stages of the game.

Returning kicks was something I had done from the moment I began playing football in the 7th grade, so it was nothing new to me. However, this appeared to be different. It was the first time our opponents lined up in punt formation to kick the ball to us in the game in which I was playing on the varsity as a freshman.

I remember jogging back to line up to receive the kick thinking to myself that my head coach had lost his mind, putting me, a freshman, back to return the kick. I recall thinking to myself (little voices in my mind) "Didn't he know that six months ago, I was in the 8th grade and now I was expected to play with 17- and 18-year-old juniors and seniors?"

My mind continued to wonder. I looked up in the stands at La Grange High School, and there were several thousand people watching the game. I looked back on to the field, and when I saw the punter lined up getting ready to take the snap from the long snapper and punt the ball to me, those little voices talking to me in my mind kicked into overdrive. They were really talking to me. That's when I said a little prayer to myself. I recall saying, "Good Lord, please do not let him kick that football to me." Then I looked to my right, and my left, and then I recall saying to myself, "You know what you fool, naturally he is going to kick it to you. You're the only back here." You see I was the only player back to return the punt as a single return man. The punter took the snap and kicked a high spiraling punt down field to me. As I settled underneath the ball to catch it, I dropped it.

Four years later after receiving communication and scholarship offers from more than 100 different colleges and universities around the country in four different sports, I chose to play football at the University of Texas, at Austin. My dream of playing college football had become a reality.

I became a starter right away as a defensive back. And in the very first game I played in DKR-Texas Memorial Stadium, my coach put me back to return a punt. As I was jogging back to line up to field the ball, I had a flashback to the same situation during my freshman year at La Grange High School.

I then looked up in the stands and instead of several thousand people watching the game, there were thousands of Texas Longhorns' fans watching the game. I looked back on to the field, and when I saw the punter lined up getting ready to take the snap from the long snapper and punt the ball to me, those little voices began talking to me in my mind. I remember thinking to myself, "Where have I seen this picture before?" That's when I said a little prayer to myself. My prayer was "Good Lord, please do not let him kick that football to me." Then I looked to my right, and my left, and then I recall saying to myself, "You know what you fool, here you go again, naturally he is going to kick it to you, you're the only back here."

You see I was the only player back to return the punt as a single return man once again. The punter took the snap and kicked a high spiraling punt down field to me. As I settled underneath the ball to catch it, I dropped the punt.

Four years later I became a #1 draft pick of the Los Angeles Rams in the National Football League. My dream of playing in the NFL had become a reality. In my very first home game with the Rams, a preseason game, my coach decided to put me back to return a punt.

As I was jogging back to line up to field the punt, I recall those little voices in my mind running rapid once again. I remember thinking to myself, "I have seen this picture twice before." I had a flashback to the same situation during my freshman year at La Grange High School and my freshman year at the University of Texas.

I then looked up in the stands and instead of seeing thousands of Texas Longhorns' fans, I saw thousands of Los Angeles Rams' fans. I looked back on to the field and when I saw the punter lined up getting ready to take the snap from the long snapper and punt the ball to me, I remember saying to myself, "Good Lord you have failed me twice before, please do not let him kick that ball to me." Then I looked to my right, and my left, and then I recall saying to myself, "You know what you fool, naturally he is going to kick it to you, you're the only back here." I was the only player back to return the punt as a single return man once again. The punter took the snap and kicked a high spiraling punt down field to me. As I settled underneath the ball to catch it, I dropped that punt as well.

Let's look at this for a moment. During each new phase of my football career, one of my big dreams had become a reality. And on each occasion the first time I had an opportunity to take steps to use more of my full potential and achieve my goals at the next level, I had a setback — I dropped the punt.

The first question I had to ask myself was could I safely field punts? The answer was yes. In fact, I could do so without a doubt. So much so that my coaches at each level had enough confidence in my ability to do so that they put me in the game as the punt returner in the very first game I played in at each new phase of my football career.

I could field punts so well that I would often field hundreds of balls each week in practice without dropping one. The question was what caused me to drop the ball at each new level I appeared? The answer was my comfort zone. I felt comfortable fielding punts in practice but not so much the first time I did so in a game at each new phase of my football career. I was out of my comfort zone.

So, have you ever asked yourself, "Why do I sometimes feel right at home in certain situations or settings but at other times I am uptight, tense, and uncomfortable? What's the problem? Is it the situation, or is it me?" The answer is simple: When we're tense and uptight, we're out of our comfort zone.

Our comfort zone is any time or place where we feel comfortable, calm, and relaxed. It's regulated by our self-image. If we see ourselves as capable, confident, and able to adapt to any situation, our comfort zone will be very far-reaching. If our dominant self-image is one of self-doubt, inferiority, and incompetence, we will have a narrower and more confining comfort zone.

Whenever we try to operate outside of our comfort zone without first expanding our self-image, our performance suffers. That was certainly the case with me trying to field a punt in my very first football game at each phase of my football career. It was also the case when I first tried making sales calls in real estate.

You may recall my sharing with you what happened to me when I first got into real estate. One day I was making sales calls, and when I asked a prospective customer if he was interested in selling his home and he said, "No, not at all, however I'm interested in purchasing a new home before the end of the year."

I promptly said to him, "Ok, thank you very much," and hung up the phone on him.

When you look at my dropping the punt at each new phase of my football career and my hanging up on a potential new customer when they needed my services in real estate, you can see I was definitely out of my comfort zone on each occasion. And my performance suffered as result.

When we find ourselves out of our comfort zone, we become so full of anxiety that all we want to do is get back to where we feel most comfortable. That's the case, even when dreams become reality. Whether or not we desire something better, if our discomfort is so strong because we are out of our comfort zone, we merely abandon our vision and goals and return quickly to our current reality.

Let's look at comfort zones more closely. At certain times and in certain situations, we may feel uncomfortable or out of place. Perhaps we experience such discomfort when we are asked to speak in front of a group, interview for a job, make a sales call to a potential new customer, learn a new software program, or try to meet a deadline at work. Maybe we feel uncomfortable when we attend an event where we don't know anyone.

In more familiar situations, we feel relaxed, calm, and comfortable. In those situations, we feel we can be ourselves because of our self-regulating comfort zone.

For every belief we hold about ourselves in current reality, there is a corresponding comfort zone. While we're in it, we know how to behave and what is expected of us. When we're out of it, we feel anxiety and stress, and this feeling can cause us to lose focus and concentration on our goals. Our breathing may become rapid and shallow; our muscles may become tense; our voice may crack; and our ability to express ourselves in words may fail.

Our self-image operates like an automatic pilot on a boat. When we program it to operate within certain boundaries, we can walk away and leave the controls. If the boat veers slightly off course, the automatic pilot will bring it back to where it belongs, on course as programmed. It will continue to operate smoothly and automatically within the selected zone until we change the programming.

There is one exception to our comfort zone's operating in a similar manner as the automatic pilot on a boat. Instead of an automatic pilot that determines where and when we operate smoothly, we have a self-image. The higher our self-esteem and the more positive our self-image, the broader our comfort zone will be. If we are confident of our ability to adapt to new situations, we'll feel more comfortable in a variety of places. If we doubt ourselves and our capacity to handle something new or different, our comfort zone will be narrow.

So I have a comfort zone, and you have a comfort zone. Highly effective people have a comfort zone, although their comfort zones are broader than most.

How we value ourselves and how we perform are controlled by our self-image and the comfort zone we create that matches this picture. Moving out of our comfort zone causes tension and anxiety. We feel out of place, both physically and emotionally. We are unable to think and act as we normally do. This discomfort drives us to get back into the range where we feel most comfortable.

We have many comfort zones. For every self-truth we have, for each current self-image we have, there is a corresponding comfort zone. As long as we live, work, and function close to our image of ourselves, we will effectively and efficiently perform tasks and skills in this area. Performing outside of our comfort zone usually lowers our performance and causes anxiety and stress.

Feelings of stress and anxiety serve as internal subconscious regulators, causing us to get back to where we think we belong. To assist in eliminating the stress and anxiety, we can learn to visualize ourselves in a new situation. We can do this safely. We can visualize ourselves in the next income level safely and visualize ourselves leading our company into a better production level. We can visualize a higher quality in all areas of our lives.

Because of our self-image pictures and comfort zones, we automatically act as we see ourselves to be. The action is automatic, a subconscious check-and-balance system. So, if we desire to change the way we act, we start with changing the way we think, and our performance will follow. It all starts with making a commitment to take steps to move us closer to the attainment of our goals.

Making and keeping commitments plays a vital role in our ability to expand our comfort zone and the achievement of our goals.

The word *commitment* is commonly used. We often hear people ask, "Will you commit to me?" A young couple may be dating, and one or the other may comment, "I am looking for a *commitment* from you."

The simple mention of the word may make some people feel uncomfortable, especially if they feel they are not ready for the commitment being requested of them.

For some of us, putting our goals in writing is a challenge, perhaps because we believe that if we put our goals in writing, we must then commit to them, and we feel we aren't ready to commit at that level yet.

In both examples, the "commitment" poses discomfort. That's because of the possibility that the commitment will cause us to venture into unknown territory. It will cause us to venture outside of our comfort zone. The bottom line is it's necessary for us to expand our comfort zone when our dreams become a reality. In doing so, we put ourselves in a better position to achieve more of our mission, vision, purpose, and goals in life.

Start Where You Are	Success Habit Patterns	Driven by a Higher Purpose	Clarify Your Current Reality	When Vision Becomes Reality	Working from Inside Out	Slow Down Long Enough So You Can Move Faster

7

SECTION

SLOW DOWN LONG ENOUGH SO YOU CAN MOVE FASTER

In today's world we have all the resources we need at our fin-gertips to put ourselves in a position to achieve more of our goals. That's the case despite any unforeseen circumstances we may encounter along the way such as things not going as planned for us or negative comments we may hear from others that may not be aligned with our aims in life.

A lot of available resources also means a lot of information we have to sort through. With so much information flowing our way on a daily basis, all designed to assist us to be more productive in life, there will come a time when we will merely need to slow down long enough so we can move faster in life.

That is definitely the case both when we encounter many adverse circumstances and especially during natural periods of transition and change that we all journey through in our lives.

CHAPTER 28

GREAT MENTORS OR COACHES EMPOWER YOU TO BE YOUR BEST

One of the greatest benefits of working with a mentor or coach is their ability to assist us to be the best we can be. They often enable us to slow down long enough so we can move faster. With each step we take toward our goals, we move one step closer to the attainment of our overall aims in life.

One of the most noteworthy sectors of society that has a great deal of impact for us is the role teachers, coaches, and school counselors play in the development of young and adolescent children. They are instrumental in empowering children to be the best they can be. When we think back, we can often think of a teacher or coach who truly made a difference in our lives.

For many of us, realizing the benefits the role mentors played in our lives continued at the collegiate level with the aid of professors, academic counselors, or coaches. For some of us, we may be currently realizing those benefits at the college level.

For many of us, we began school as early as preschool. That's when we met our teacher for the first time. For others, we met our teacher for the first time when we started 1st grade.

On either occasion, from that point forward we benefitted from the presence of a teacher, school counselors, or an extracurricular activities coach until we graduated from high school. For those who went on to college, they continued to benefit mightily from the presence of professors, mentors and coaches in their lives at the collegiate level. And then when you stop and really think about it, the unthinkable happens.

After graduation from high school for some and college for others, many people transition to the next phase of their lives. And when they do, they leave their mentors or coaches behind. That is, unless they take steps to create a mentor or coaching relationship for everyday life when they transition to the next phase of their lives.

When you study highly effective people, many of them have relationships with mentors or personal or business coaches. This is the case regardless of what space they operate in.

Professional athletes in all sports benefit from the presence of their coaches. Actors and actresses have acting coaches. Singers have voice coaches. Business leaders have business coaches. Many highly successful people benefit from having mentors or personal or business coaches in their lives.

I've been personally coached or benefited from mentors my entire life. One of the most valued relationship I have today is with my longtime good friend and mentor Gino Blefari. Gino serves as the CEO of HSF Affiliates, which operates the real estate brokerage networks of Berkshire Hathaway HomeServices, Prudential Real Estate, and Real Living Real Estate.

The two of us come from two different backgrounds. I came from the sports world, and although Gino participated in sports in high school… ironically, he played the same position in high school that I played in the NFL, safety and cornerback … and he was even inducted into his high school Hall of Fame receiving the award of "Most Valuable Defensive Back: Two Consecutive Years," he came from the entrepreneurial and business world. Today, he serves as one of my most valued mentors, and I serve as one of his mentors.

We meet weekly for breakfast as part of our weekly routine. This is a step we've been taking for years. We cover all aspects of life when we meet. With each meeting I feel we often move one step closer to achieving more of our respective missions, visions, purposes, and goals in life. I am often inspired, encouraged, and empowered after our meetings. On many occasions, they remind me of the value and benefits of having a great mentor and coach.

If ever there was a need for great mentors and coaches, today is the day. To put it mildly, we live in a fast pace world today. One in which we have instant access to just about any product, service, or resource we desire or need to aid us in the attainment of our goals. Technology provides us with a platform on which we can meet many of our needs with the click of a button.

Technology can also provide us with many challenges, especially when we encounter circumstances that hinder our ability to remain focused on our goals. The challenges are often enhanced when we set out to achieve our goals and things end up not going as planned, or when we hear negative comments from others that are not aligned with our aims in life.

This is when we will need to be able to bring true meaning to words like courage, focus, faith, persistence, commitment, resilience, and others when we need to take that forward step. This is also when we all can benefit from having a great mentor or coach.

When we run into the normal twists, turns, and roadblocks in life, great mentors and coaches can assist us in taking steps daily to grow personally and professionally during these encounters. They can also assist us in enhancing our skill set daily, which aids us in overcoming the challenges we encounter in becoming the best we can be.

This is part of our mission and purpose at World Class Coaches. As a coaching company, we seek to take steps daily to equip people, teams, and organizations with the means to unleash more of their natural God-given potential. One of our aims is to assist you in applying the knowledge and wisdom you possess when you need to take that step and to assist you in bringing true meaning to those character words when you need to apply them in your life.

With this is mind, you may ask yourself, what is the true role of a mentor or coach? Well, the role of a World Class Coaches coach is to serve as an accountability partner to assist in improving the quality of the search in identifying and practicing the basic fundamentals of whatever trade you choose, which is necessary for a more fulfilling and satisfying future.

An accountability partner, a great mentor or coach, is able to see things you can't see when blind spots and weaknesses block your vision. Such a person serves as a resource to promote personal, professional, and spiritual growth and watches out for your best interests. In looking for this type of confidant, World Class Coaches looks for the following characteristics in a good mentor or coach:

1. Sounding Board: There are times when we all need someone to bounce things off of — we need a confidant. One of the strongest set of skills a great mentor or coach possesses is the ability "to ask the right question at the appropriate time to obtain the outcome they desire," and "to listen, hear, and understand what is being communicated to them." This process will enable them to serve as a facilitator in assisting you in arriving at your desired outcome with confidence with your mentor or coach as your guide.

2. Wise Counsel: Another vital set of skills mentors or coaches should possess is "effective communication" and "effective decision-making" skills. Regardless of circumstances, when communicating with you

they should offer genuine wisdom based on solid principles and fundamentally sound business practices.

3. Trustworthy: Trust is a vital component of any relationship. It is extremely important as an accountability partner. Your mentor or coach should keep things shared by you in the strictest of confidence, unless they are otherwise requested or required to share it.

4. Accepting: The goal in working with you is not to create a flawless individual. Your mentor or coach should allow you to be yourself -- frailties and all -- and not try to remake you into a "perfect" person.

5. Courageous: We all can benefit from someone who is able to say what we need to hear when we need to hear it without making us feel helpless or criticized. Your mentor or coach should take steps to "compassionately" confront you with the truth, even when it's uncomfortable.

6. Forgiving: None of us is perfect. You will make mistakes, and your mentor or coach will make mistakes. Build trust through mutual forgiveness.

7. Edifying: On occasion you may be vulnerable to feeling insignificant. You may even be in need of being edified. A great mentor or coach has a "sincere" way to edify you.

8. Encouraging: Great mentors or coaches do not judge you or anyone. Their goal should not be to have a checklist and act as if they are prophets. They should take great joy in encouraging, inspiring, and empowering you to be the best you can be. A mentor or coach's role is to serve as an accountability partner to assist you in consistently taking steps to use more of your full God-given

potential. This process will enable you to take steps daily in practicing the basic fundamentals of your chosen career, both personally and professionally, and to put you in the best position for success in meeting your needs and achieving your goals.

When working with a great mentor or coach, you can express your needs and desires clearly and behave in ways that respect the needs of others without sacrificing your own needs or lowering your standards. Working with a mentor or coach enables you to say "no" when others are saying "yes" to things that are not in alignment with their mission, vision, purpose, goals, and values. He or she enables you to safely take the risks you need to take in order to grow and remain focused on your goals.

Great mentors and coaches provide you with the freedom to develop and utilize more of your full potential. They provide you with a platform to admit your mistakes and weaknesses and develop a proactive approach to be the best you can be. Being your best means you move closer to achieving your goals in life.

CHAPTER 29

SELF-CONFIDENCE IN THE EYE OF A STORM

There's something special about being at our best when we find ourselves in the eye of a storm. The more confident we are in pursuing our goals, the more likely we will utilize more of our God-given potential and will move closer to achieving more of our overall mission, vision, purpose, and goals in life.

Webster's dictionary defines self-confidence as, "Belief in oneself and one's powers or abilities." In order to consistently put ourselves in the best position for success in achieving our overall aims in life, there's a need for us to consistently grow personally and professionally. This includes being on a constant search in seeking ways to improve our focus and confidence in our lives. We work on improving ourselves from the inside. We learn to focus our time, efforts, and energies within our circle of focus. If something falls in our area of no control, we do not focus any of our time or efforts on it.

However, at one time or another in our lives, we may feel that we have the ideal plan and are taking all the right steps, but the results we desire are nowhere to be found. We try to remain focused and confident in our goals; however, we're simply not realizing the results we're looking for. We may then ask ourselves, "How much longer can I stay with this plan because it's not working for me?"

When this happens, it's normal for us to suffer a loss of self-confidence. Our loss of confidence may hinder our ability to remain focused on consistently practicing the necessary fundamentals of our profession, although we know that's what we should be doing. We may even indulge in self-pity and play the role of the victim.

When twists, turns, roadblocks, or tough circumstances show up in our lives, they can cause us to question our ability to be the best we can be. They also can leave us asking the question: "Why me?" The storms in our lives can test the depth of our faith and confidence. When our faith and confidence are being tested, there are usually three primary areas we tend to question:

1. **We question ourselves.** We begin to ask ourselves if we have what it takes to achieve our desired goals in life, or if we even want them if we do realize them. We lose faith and confidence in ourselves.

2. **We question the process.** We begin to have questions about the process or systems we're utilizing to achieve our desired results. We begin to look at all those things outside of us, looking for ways to effectively deal with the challenges in our lives.

3. **We question the presence of God.** We ask ourselves, "Why me?" We may feel that we've had our fair share of storms in life and wonder why we are still encountering life challenges.

God has a plan for each of us, and it has not changed. Maybe we've encountered a storm in our lives, and if we are able to turn the circumstances surrounding the storm over to God and refocus on those things we have control over in our lives we can begin the process of regaining faith and confidence in ourselves and the process we're utilizing to realize our aims in life. By taking proactive steps to overcome the circumstances we encounter in life, we may encounter special blessings just around the corner.

This leads us to the question, "What is an ideal state of mind to consistently perform at our best, regardless of the circumstances we find ourselves in?" For highly effective people, it's a combination of being focused and energized yet calm, cool, confident, and faithful to their goals that creates an ideal state of mind to perform at their best.

What separates the world-class performers from others who perform at a lower level? Some of the reasons include their ability to maintain the ideal state of mind for a longer period of time and their ability to not allow the normal twists, turns, and roadblocks that enter their lives to hinder their focus or self-confidence.

As we journey through life, we encounter tough circumstances, things not going as planned, and we hear negative comments from others that are not in alignment with our aims. These circumstances create obstacles and barriers in our lives. They add chaos to a life already filled with circumstances we cannot control. How calm, cool, confident, and faithful we remain while in the storm will determine how well we remain focused on our goals. And it will affect our state of mind and performance.

We may not really know the depth of our faith or the degree of our self-confidence until we find ourselves in the midst of a storm. We may never know these things unless we find ourselves in a situation where we are put to the test. How we react at those moments will provide us with a glimpse of how we really see ourselves on the inside and the depth of our faith. This is when we see a preview of our true subconscious beliefs.

During storms, our deep-seated beliefs and true character traits rise to the surface. At such times, our ability to remain focused, energized, faithful, calm, cool, and confident is tested. This is when we come to know whether we truly believe who we say we are as a person or whether we've only been pretending to be someone or something on the outside we're not on the inside. Adversity reveals the true subconscious character of a person.

People operating with an ideal mind set perform more consistently over time, remain more focused on their goals, and approach life with more drive, energy, and motivation. The more focused, calm, cool, and confident we are in pursuing our goals and living our lives, the more likely we are to remain focused on our goals, while others may be easily hindered by the challenges they encounter in life. This approach will better enable us to remain self-confident in the eye of a storm.

CHAPTER 30

FAITH PROVIDES A PLATFORM FOR POSITIVE EXPECTATIONS

People with a positive expectation of life have a tendency to have things go well for them. Those who expect the best tend to get it. They expect life to go well for them, and it usually does.

When they run into twists, turns, or roadblocks along the way, they persist in their efforts because they expect to succeed in the end. They seem to learn from encountering setbacks or past experiences, and they are stronger and more resilient as a result. They succeed because they know they deserve it. And they affirm themselves by saying things like "That's like me!"

Highly effective people who consistently utilize more of their God-given potential have a success habit pattern of using positive self-talk to build and reinforce an already positive self-image. They expect the best!

On the flip side, people who are constantly expecting the worst or failure seem to get what they expect as well. When things are going well for them, they worry about when obstacles or barriers will appear again. When they fail, they're not surprised because they've been expecting it all along. If they happen to succeed, they attribute it to luck, and they quickly return to their usual poor performance and say to themselves: "That's just like me."

When storms blow into our lives from all directions, our faith is tested, and we may be tempted to give up on our goals.

However, it is at this point at which we can learn a great deal from observing highly effective people. As focused and confident as they may be, when they encounter some of these forces in their lives, they tend to turn to a higher power, their faith in God, to help them through. They do all they can do within their power to overcome the challenges standing between them and their aims in life; however, if they feel that the problem is bigger than they are, they turn it over to God. They then focus their time, effort, and energies on areas over which they have control. They allow God to do His best work over the things they have no control over.

The decision to turn things over which they have no control over to God puts them in a better position to be the best that they can be. Their faith enables them to remain focused on the things they have control of and to remain connected to their mission, vision, purpose, goals, and values in life.

This alignment will take us a long way in life — up to the point where God may step into our lives and test the depth of our faith.

Let's look at the *biblical* definition of faith in Hebrews 11:1: "Faith is the substance of things hoped for, the evidence of things not seen." So, having faith means believing in something without seeing it.

Often, if we're looking for a reason to justify our failure to achieve our goals, we will find it — there is a reason and an excuse around every corner. We encounter difficult situations every day that can lead to a storm.

For many of us, the road from current reality to our aims in life is long and filled with obstacles. Some of these obstacles show up in the form of things not going as planned based on our expectations, causing us to question everything from ourselves to the methods and plans we use to achieve our goals. On occasion, the storms we run into in life will be so powerful that they stop us squarely in our tracks. Such moments of truth will test our faith.

While we can't control many of the circumstances in our lives, we can learn to control our reaction to them and our self-talk. We can learn to think and talk to ourselves in ways that will make us much more effective. We can learn to expect the best. When we do, we will be able to utilize more of our full potential and remain focused on our goals while in the storm.

Expecting the best affirms that we have confidence in ourselves and faith in God to handle those things that are out of our control. Expecting the best enhances our belief in ourselves as well as our abilities to meet challenges and deal constructively with obstacles and barriers in life.

When something happens that we don't expect, we are confident enough to handle it. If we find ourselves in the midst of challenges, even very serious ones, we know we can weather the storm. We pick ourselves up, dust ourselves off, and start all over again, knowing that we've gained knowledge and wisdom from the experience and that we have what it takes to succeed. When a challenge seems bigger than we are, we don't quit on our goal, we turn it over to God.

When we expect the best, we affirm our ability to remain focused on our goals. Expecting the best means becoming solution-focused instead of problem-focused. We don't spend much time thinking about what's wrong. Instead, we acknowledge the problems, analyze them, and focus our mental energy on what we want it to look like when the problem is resolved.

Many things in this world are beyond your control; I encourage you to turn those things over to God. But there is one very important thing that we have total control over, and that is what goes into our mind. We can take charge of our thoughts and self-talk. We can make sure that our self-talk consists of a hopeful, confident, self-affirming expectation of a future we can get excited about.

When we exercise control over our self-talk, we build a positive self-image that will create opportunities, open doors, and move mountains, enabling us to remain energized, calm, cool, confident, faithful, and focused when we encounter storms in life.

POSTSCRIPT

PROBLEM-SOLVER FOR LIFE

I feel blessed in life. Many of the reasons why revolve around the life experiences that have inspired my mission, vision, and purpose in life.

Life is a process of continuous transition and change. When the time arises we naturally move to the next phase of our lives, whether we're ready for it or not. There are many factors that drive these natural changes in our lives or the lives of our loved ones. Some of them can potentially pose a risk to us achieving our goals in life.

Goal attainment is a process driven by a higher purpose. In pursuit of our purpose, we achieve our goals, one step at a time. Often, it requires us to have a purpose-driven platform and the focus and direction that will enable us to take the first step, then the next step, one at a time to put ourselves in position to achieve our goals.

So when we encounter obstacles or barriers in life, they are not problems, as long as we can do something about it. The question is what are we going to do about it?

Well, we're going to become a problem-solver for life. We will take steps to apply our knowledge and wisdom when needed to move one step closer to achieving our goals. We will take steps to tap into our healthy competitive spirit and apply true meaning to words like courage, faith, persistence, forgiveness, resilience, and others when needed to assist us around, over, or through any obstacles or barriers we encounter that may hinder our path to the attainment of our goals.

As we apply these principles consistently we will see positive changes in our lives. We will feel more powerful than we have ever felt before, and we will move one step closer to the attainment of our overall goals whether we realize it or not.

As a focused, fearless, and faithful person, we will feel more confident about bringing our mission, vision, purpose, goals, and values for the future into reality. With God's guidance, we will have a growing sense of being in control of our own lives. It won't happen like magic overnight, but it will happen.

We now have the knowledge that, if we consistently apply our skills and remain confident, we will remain focused on our goals, even when we encounter adverse or negative circumstances.

When we take full accountability for our own lives and consistently follow the steps I have outlined, there are no limits to what we can accomplish in life. We also have what it takes to inspire and encourage others in ways that allow them to rise above self-doubt and pursue their own greatest ambitions without focusing on the limitations set by others.

This doesn't mean our lives will become a fairy tale fantasy. We will still experience some challenges, obstacles, barriers, roadblocks, or setbacks along the way. There will likely be times when we'll wonder if our goals are too high. At other times we may be tempted to give up and quit. No doubt, there will be times when our commitments to our goals will waiver. But these are the times when this information will become even more valuable. If we maintain the faith when we encounter many of these difficulties and obstacles that we run into in life, we gain additional knowledge and wisdom to better enable us to realize more of our aims in life.

We can't control everything that happens in our lives, but we can control our response to what happens. We can become a problem-solver when we run into obstacles or barriers in life. Every setback we face can be turned into a springboard with the knowledge and wisdom we gain with each one we overcome. Tough times can make us stronger. We can weather any storm and be a better person as a result if we control our self-talk and keep our mission, vision, purpose, goals, and values in focus and be accountable for our actions during the tough times.

The tools we now have available to us and the knowledge we now possess are powerful. But if we don't use them, we won't succeed. If we do use them, setbacks may still occur, but we'll see them as temporary and find our way around, over or through them.

The more of our God-given potential we use daily, the more we can help other people grow and deal more effectively with the challenges they may face. When we share what we learn with others, we show them we believe in their ability to grow and be the best they can be.

When we remind them of their strengths and potential, we'll be a powerful force in developing them to be the best they can be. We'll help them to believe in themselves and utilize more of their gifts and potential. And we'll help the world be a more productive and better place to live for all of us. With each step taken, we move closer to the achievement of our overall goals.

MOVING FAMILIES INITIATIVE EXTRACURRICULAR ACTIVITIES SCHOLARSHIP PLAN

WORLD CLASS COACHES

World Class Coaches is an international personal, professional, and executive coaching company that practices and teaches basic fundamentals as part of its coaching delivery processes. The company coaches across all industry lines.

> "Our mission is to empower individuals to achieve their God-given potential and significantly increase their performance capability by recognizing their ability to choose personal and professional growth in order to achieve personal and professional excellence."

The company provides world-class coaching programs, seminars, workshops, and consulting services that enhance personal and organizational performance in the areas of sales, leadership, teamwork, communication, motivation, and life management skills. To inquire about coaching programs or to schedule a guest speaker, contact us at:

World Class Coaches
2300 W. Sahara Ave. #800
Las Vegas, NV 89102
www.movingfamiliesinitiative.com
www.worldclasscoaches.com
800-314-7713
Fax 702-920-7655
wccinfo@worldclasscoaches.com